Another Book
of Mormon

Jay Craig

Copyright © 2015 by Jay Craig

Jay Craig/Kenneth Craig Publishing Company
5320 28th Ave NW
Ballard, WA 98107
scottishbuddhism.com

CULTURE

Jay Craig's work was supported by an Artist Project grant from 4Culture of King County, Washington. Peggy Sturdivant is also partly responsible for this book.

the Scottish Buddhist Cookbook, Another Book of Mormon/Jay Craig
 -- 1st ed.
ISBN 978-0-692-57123-1

Ride the Duck

It was about four or five in the morning and I hadn't slept in a couple of days. I'd been cycling back and forth pretty hard between mania and depression for a few weeks and didn't have the attention span to accomplish much more than surfing around online.

I had some work but it was menial so I looked up jobs on CraigsList. And there, right in front of me, was a job listing for Ride the Ducks of Seattle. It actually said, "Do your friends think your crazy?" (Yes.) Has anyone in your family tried to get you committed? (Maybe.) "Well then, you should be a Duck Captain!"

The idea of me being a Duck Captain was so absurd it made perfect sense. I imagined telling my friends that I was applying and having a good laugh over it. My only experience so far with the Ducks was watching them drive around like a bunch of idiots, dancing to 'YMCA' and blasting their kazoos, and that's not me at all. And I've never been much of a people person. I prefer dogs. I might be a horrible captain, but I like to write and I'm always on the lookout for new material, so I applied.

I asked a couple friends to write me a reference and Peggy hesitated. If some Duck-hating local pushed my buttons, could she be sure I wouldn't drive us all over an embankment? I assured her there was no liability involved, but to be honest, I wasn't really sure.

She knew my story as well as anybody. I told her how once, in the depths of my depression, I went downtown begging for help from Summit Research Center, which specializes in treating bipolar disorder. The intake woman never even made eye contact with me as she read over my patient form. "You drink a six-pack of beer a night? You're an alcoholic. Go to AA and come back when you're clean."

I didn't fight it. I didn't ask her if she knew what self-medication is. I just got in my car and drove to the Aurora Bridge to throw my sorry ass off.

But the Aurora Bridge is no longer very suitable for throwing your sorry ass off. There's no place to park and now there's a suicide fence to climb over. The traffic was too heavy for me to stop so I got off and turned around but didn't have any luck going Southbound either, so I just went back to my shop and rode out the storm for a couple months.

Fortunately, my friend believed in helping out a manic depressive more than the clinic did and she wrote me a great reference.

Ride the Ducks called me in for an interview and it went well. The managers seemed like good guys and they liked the fact that I was up on current events. They sent me out on a Duck ride to get an idea of what I'd be doing if I got hired. The captain was a jerk but I thought it would be cool to drive a WWII amphibious landing vehicle around Seattle and into Lake Union. "I can do better than this guy," I thought. Besides, I told people I was going to be a Duck Captain. So screw it, I went to the audition.

The audition did not go well. I was very nervous being up in front of a bunch of people and being forced to do improve. I hate improve. It's the lowest form of comedy. There were five other applicants and we were all made to do acting games and play with props like it was some kind of hazing. It was horrible.

I got a call the next day from one of the managers who told me that of the eight people in the jury, four voted for me, and four against. Hung jury. He asked if I'd be willing to come in and audition again. "Yes!" I said, automatically and enthusiastically. "Sounds like fun!"

Then I did something I've never done before. I went to the nearest mirror and stared at myself, wondering, Who are you?

But it was very important that I get this job. It was a test I needed to pass. The second audition was a week away so I bought some tooth whitener and practiced smiling. I went to the store and practiced my improv. "Does this can of tuna make my ass look fat?", I asked some old guy. "Check out these tomatoes!", I told some girl in the produce section while holding up a couple ripe ones.

I worked on my intro and taught myself to play 'Amazing Grace' on the kazoo since I thought I'd have a Scottish theme going on. At the next audition they ate it up and I got the job. Seattle, meet your newest tour guide- Captain Braveliver!

In my first week of running tours, I was nervously going over my intro and looking at my cheat sheet. Two minutes before I was supposed to start my tour, I was told that the boarding crew had accidently loaded up Captain Rick O'Shea's private charter on my Duck and put the public tour on his.

"What? What does that mean?"

"It means you have a whole Duck full of 15-year-olds from Yakima. They just graduated from middle school and they're pumped up. Go!"

My tour is all about history and my jokes are aimed at adults so I had absolutely no idea what to do. They were gonna HATE me. I asked Captain Rick what I should do and he told me to just blast some music and I'd be fine.

As I got out to the Duck I was horrified. It was completely full of teenagers and every one of them had a quacker, those obnoxious noisemakers that the owners of the Ducks seem to think make for a better experience.

I walked up the aisle knowing full well these kids would not appreciate my intro or how much it actually rains in Seattle (36 inches, less than Houston, New Orleans, Miami, Philadelphia, New York and Boston). These kids wanted to party and they got stuck with Captain Braveliver, worst Duck Capatain ever.

The noise was deafening- 'QUACK! QUACK! QUACK! QUACK! QUACK! QUACK! QUACK!'

"HEY, EVERYBODY!", I yelled. "ARE YOU READY TO GO FOR A DUCK RIDE?"

'QUACK! QUACK! QUACK! QUACK!'

"I SAID, ARE YOU READY TO GO FOR A FREAKING DUCK RIDE?!? WOOOOOOOOOO!!!!!"

'QUACK! QUACK! QUACK! QUACK! QUACK! QUACK! QUACK! QUACK! QUACK!!!!!!'

I skipped past the regular intro and went right into the safety stuff. I just wanted to get out on the road and get this thing over with. If they complained to management, fine. I was not cut out for this. Thirty seconds into going over the explanation of what you should do if we started to sink, I gave up. They could figure out how to don a life jacket themselves. Or not.

I told them they had to sit down but they wouldn't stop quacking. The four chaperones had their hands over their ears and I lost it.

"HEY! YOU KNOW WHAT THOSE QUACK-ERS ARE? THOSE ARE SOUVENIRS! YOU KNOW WHAT YOU DO WITH A SOUVENIR? YOU PUT IT IN YOUR POCKET TIL YOU GET HOME!!"

I yelled, "I SWEAR TO GOD IF I HEAR ONE MORE QUACK OUT OF YOU KIDS I'M GONNA DRIVE US ALL RIGHT INTO THE LAKE!!!"

And they were all like, 'YAY! QUACK! QUACK! QUACK! QUACK! QUACK! QUACK!'

The principal, who was sitting in the front row, said, "Man, I wish I could yell at the them like that!"

I blasted some bagpipe music and quickly realized these kids didn't expect anything out of me. Hormones were raging. Nobody cared about the old fart driving and they certainly didn't want to hear any history.

But I couldn't let them win so I turned off the music and condensed my 90 minute tour down to fifteen seconds- "WHEN THEY FIRST SETTLED SEATTLE THEY BUILT THIS CITY ON THE BEACH! IT KEPT FLOODING AND THERE WAS SEWAGE EVERY-WHERE! IT WAS INFESTED WITH RATS, THE PEOPLE WERE UGLY, SEATTLE SUCKED! SEATTLE WAS A DUMP! AND THEN ONE DAY THE WHOLE CITY BURNED DOWN! SO THEY REBUILT IT AND RAISED IT UP TWENTY FEET! AND THEN THERE WAS A GOLD RUSH BUT THERE WASN'T MUCH GOLD AND THE ONLY PEOPLE WHO MADE MONEY WERE THE PEOPLE SELLING THE SHOV-ELS!"

I set the music to full blast and we all PUT OUR HANDS UP IN THE AIR SOMETIMES, SAYING, HEY OH! GOTTA LET GO!

The kids got off the Duck high-fiving me and tell-ing me I was the best Duck Captain EVER and the adults tipped me $60. I passed.

I survived. We all survived. Going over the Aurora Bridge and everything.

On one of my last days driving a Duck, I pulled up to the boat ramp with a full load of passengers. The ramp was crowded with Duck-hating locals launching and haul-ing out their boats. The first thing you do at the ramp is look down the channel to see if there are any other Ducks coming and check out who's doing what with their boats.

There was another Duck halfway up the channel, ready to land, and a truck with a powerboat on the ramp ready to launch as soon as the Duck got out of the water.

I pulled up alongside the powerboat. Onboard was an older woman who, before I even came to a stop, started yelling at me. "NO! No way! We were here first! You're just gonna have to wait for us!"

I started to tell her that I was all ready to go and could be in the water and out of her life in about fifteen seconds. But she started screaming, "NO! I hate you Ducks! Always driving around going, Quack! Quack! Quack! You can just sit here! In fact, you tell your boss I said, blah blah blah blah blah."

There were many ways I could go on this one. But there was something I taught myself early on as a way to manage my roller coaster emotions. It's okay to think whatever I want, but it's my actions that will get me into trouble. As long as I take a breath and don't lose my cool, I'll be fine. Don't do the first thing that comes into your head, do the second.

So I've got this lady yelling at me in front of my passengers and I can't yell back at her, and I kind of sympathize with her, but still, I have to say something so instead of blowing up on her I pull out my inner Scottish Buddhist- "Mom! You're embarrassing me in front of my passengers!"

She just looks at me, dumbfounded, so I yell, "You promised you'd stop doing this to me!"

Her mouth hung open but nothing came out.

Her husband, in the truck, busted up laughing and as the other Duck was driving up the ramp, he waved me ahead.

My passengers all yelled, "Yay!" and started quacking and I heard the women scream, "Goddamnit Harold! You know how I feel about those things!" as we drove past them and into the water.

There's a moment when the Duck's wheels submerge and the lumbering WWII relic floats quietly before the engine is engaged.

I felt a little proud of myself. Not just for my new-found restraint, but for everything it took to even get this job. Managing a mental disorder can be as difficult as managing a physical one. There was a time I didn't trust my life in my own hands, now even a teenager with a quacker was safe with me. It suddenly seemed that becoming a Duck Captain was one of the smartest things I'd ever done. To celebrate, I let us drift quietly for a minute.

Tomato Soup

Every time you take the lid off to smell what's in the crock pot it takes, I've heard, an additional 15-20 minutes to regain the heat. Not such a big deal with the tomato soup, but it's a good thing to know, especially with the lasagna.

Needed-
Butter
2 onions
Garlic
6-8 large tomatoes
Flour
Salt and pepper
Oregano, if you have it
Tabasco

Prepare the Pot (see page 18)

Dice the fresh tomatoes. Combine with some more butter, the second onion (diced), a little flour, and the spices in the crock pot.

Turn the pot to **Low** and cook for 5 to 8 hours.

Suggested beverage- Pike Place Pale Ale.

'Hi! I'm Maggie!'

It was late December, 2001, when I came home wearing a kilt and ceremoniously threw all my pants in the dumpster, declaring, "I'm never wearing pants again!" By New Years Eve, Vanessa decided to leave me.

I had argued against a divorce initially because we got along so well and I was unprepared to cook for myself. But ten years was a long time to be married, so we split amicably. We got her an apartment in the building we were in so we could share custody of our dog, Chloe, and she was out within two weeks. We agreed that I would help her set up her new place and she would make sure I was eating properly. And we'd get together for regular sex, at least until one of us started seeing somebody.

We spent most of a Sunday morning moving her stuff (or half of our stuff) into her new apartment. Our neighbor across the hall was in and out all day and knew what was going on. She made an effort to talk to both me and Vanessa, being all Sad and There For Us.

Rachael's cute and she's always been a little flirty with me. At one point when Vanessa wasn't around, Rachael told me she was going in for breast reduction surgery in a couple months. I said, "Oh, really? I'm thinking of getting penis reduction surgery. Maybe we could get together for a little 'before and after'."

She looked down and I really thought she was gonna lift up my kilt to check for herself, but she just smiled at me and I said she should come over later and have a glass of wine on our porch (she was always envious of our porch). She said, "Maybe" and went back into her apartment. I hadn't been with anybody but Vanessa since we got married, and I wasn't necessarily thinking I was gonna get Rachael into bed that night, but I thought it would be good to have somebody cute to talk to. Maybe have her over a couple times and see what happens.

We moved up all of Vanessa's stuff and it got down to the last bag of books. She set it down and gave me a hug. "I know this is the right thing to do. We'll be fine," she said. "Who knows? Maybe we just need some time apart."

As she was hugging me, I could tell she was crying. She later told me that she'd spent the night up in her new place going through all our pictures, listening to the music we both liked, and wondering if this was all a mistake.

It was a pretty long hug. Long enough for me to realize that I was about to spend my first night alone. Ten years of marriage, over and done. I didn't really want to be alone. I'd always preferred having a partner, I function better that way. And now I have to start dating again. Well, I thought, there's no shortage of cute girls in this town, that's for sure. There's the cutie who serves me coffee in the morning, of course, and the blonde teller at my bank, Sara. There was Amy who worked at the marina, and Lisa who worked at the boat brokerage I sometimes did jobs for. There was Theresa who lived in Boston, maybe I could fly her out for a weekend. There was the waitress at the Hilltop, the chick over at Ken's Market, and that other waitress at the Hilltop, the one with the short blonde hair and green eyes. Goddamn, I'd LOVE to fuck that one. And Rachael. Maybe I WILL try to do her tonight, I thought.

Vanessa let go of me, gave me a kiss good-bye, grabbed her books, and she and Chloe were gone. I closed the door, had a beer and wondered what the hell I was going to do with the rest of my life. Vanessa claimed she loved me, she was just having a hard time dealing with my bipolar disorder, so she left. And here I was, alone.

But it was still early on Sunday afternoon and I had a couple hours before I was gonna invite Rachael over drinks and hopefully some naked time, so naturally, I went out for a beer.

I decided to go up to a place on Phinney Ridge that I had been to a week before. I had gone there for several years for my buddy Dave's annual birthday party, and the week before was the first one we had after he had died, a few months earlier. And that was the first time I'd worn my new kilt out to a bar. I had gone without Vanessa, as she was protesting the kilt. The cute waitress, however, was drawn to it immediately and couldn't keep her fingers off of it. Being married, I didn't really flirt back, but I relished the positive reinforcement that you need when you first start wearing a skirt out in public.

I had a beer, but the cute waitress wasn't there. I wrote a note on the back of my business card, something to the effect of- 'Hey! Remember me? I'm the guy in the Utilikilt from last week. I was married then, but now I'm not! Wanna get together?' I gave it to the bartender and asked her to give it to the girl who was working last Saturday night- dark hair, cute. I think she said she likes to paint...? [She never did call]

I finished my beer, and I was pretty low. For some reason I thought I'd run into this waitress and she'd be so happy I was now single, she'd invite me back to her place. We would get some red wine, paint each other's naked bodies, and fuck all night. It seemed reasonable enough but it wasn't happening.

Plan B-

I got in the truck and drove back to Queen Anne. Basically to park 'cause I was gonna go get smashed at one of the bars within stumbling distance to home. If I was gonna spend the night alone, I wasn't gonna do it sober, that was for damn sure.

I went to Hoyt's and had a few beers and shots of scotch up at the bar. At some point I saw a group of four college-aged girls playing pool, so I ordered up a pitcher, got four more glasses and sat down at their booth. Before I could think of something witty to say (I should have thought of something before I went over there), they grabbed their drinks and moved everything to a new table. Fine. More beer for me.

Sometime after that I felt somebody sit down on the bench next to me and was relieved to find it was an attractive woman. "Hi! I'm Maggie!" she said, with an adorable English accent. My spirits rose.

We drank beer and whisky and she seemed to actually care about this drunk, pathetic guy whose wife just left him. She told me I didn't have to spend the night alone, and came back to my place.

We went to my apartment and drank and smoked and blasted music and fucked. I don't remember thinking anything about it. I don't recall even thinking about Vanessa as I was boning Maggie. I don't think I even felt relief that I could still get laid after all those years of monogamy. I just needed some human contact.

At seven in the morning my alarm went off, and although I'd barely even closed my eyes and was still kind of drunk, I knew I had to get to work by eight otherwise my guys would stand around doing nothing, or worse, do something stupid.

My head was killing me, there was a naked chick next to me who was not my wife, and I had to take a dump. I drank some water and went and sat on the toilet. I had my head in my hands, and was trying to get a grasp on what had happened in the last twenty-four hours when the naked woman comes bouncing into the bathroom and jumps in the shower. I started to point out that I was sitting on the toilet over here, and she said, "Oh, just strike a match, love." It was the English chick.

I sat there knowing that something was very wrong, but I couldn't figure out what it was. My mind was a blur and I tried to methodically recreate the events of the last several hours. It was very difficult and I couldn't quite get clarity.

Until I heard the unmistakable jingle of Chloe's collar as she came bounding up the stairs outside the apartment and I remember that I was supposed to take her for the day so she wouldn't have to spend it in Vanessa's new apartment all alone. Seconds later I hear keys opening the front door and it's much too late (and quite inconvenient) for me to try and close the bathroom door.

My now-very-certainly-ex-wife-to-be pauses outside the bathroom and sees me on the crapper. She notices the shower running and gives me a puzzled look. Before she has a chance to ask me why the hell I have the shower going, the curtain swings open and the naked English chick says, "Hi! I'm Maggie!"

Vanessa turned and left. Which was a good thing 'cause I got the impression that Maggie was all up for a dripping wet conversation with the woman she'd heard so much about the night before.

Weeks later, when Vanessa was talking to me again, she admitted that Maggie had given her the closure that years of therapy might not have provided, and she thanked me.

Meatloaf

Meatloaf is a staple of the Scottish Buddhist diet.

Needed-
Butter
Onions
Garlic
5 pounds ground beef
2 pieces of toast
6 eggs
Oregano, if you have it
Salt and pepper
Cheddar cheese
Precooked bacon
Heinz catsup

Prepare the Pot (see page 18)

Chop up the second onion and some more garlic and add to a large bowl.

Wash your hands again, remove the lid from the crock pot, and stir the butter, onion and garlic around the pot, buttering the sides.

Add in the ground beef, eggs, toast, oregano (if you have it), and salt and pepper to the large bowl. Mix together well, lift out of the bowl, bouncing it around to pack it all together, and drop it into the crock pot. Press the center down making it concave. This will help later. Turn the pot to **Low** and cook for 4 hours.

Remove the coagulated fat and grease and turn the pot to High for 2 hours.

Remove more fat and grease, and add the bacon, cheese and catsup, and cook on **Low** for a couple more hours.

Serve with chilled catsup.

Suggested beverage- Fremont Universale Pale in a can.

All Scottish Buddhist crock pot meals are begun in the same way-

Preparing the Pot

<u>Needed-</u>
Crock Pot
A large pat of butter
One onion
One bulb of garlic
Wooden spoon

Turn the crock pot to **High** and drop in the butter. Mince up garlic, chop the onion, and add to the pot.
Stir occasionally while preparing
the other ingredients.

NOTE- Margarine does not work.
If you're so worried about your weight,
eat smaller servings, fat-ass.

Suggested beverage- Pike Place Pale Ale.

St Bernard's

We actually had a great marriage, Vanessa and I. But not once, not one single time for the entirety of our ten-year marriage, not ONCE, did we have a meaningful conversation about religion.

On our very first date we had dinner and then went to visit my Nana so we could sneak up on the roof of her tall apartment building with a bottle of wine.

Sitting out on the ledge, looking up at the stars, I asked Vanessa if she believed in God. But before she could answer I launched into a tirade about organized religion and how the whole concept of God is ridiculous.

After I made my lengthy case, I again asked her if she was religious. She took a swig of wine and said, "I don't think I want to talk about religion with you." So we never did. Not once.

Which drove me crazy because religion is my favorite topic. I grew up going to church and I graduated from Catholic high school an atheist with a degree in pointless religious debate. But at least I had fun. Private school is full of good drugs and top quality fake IDs and everything you've heard about Catholic girls is correct.

When I was a sophomore Dean Powers had asked me if I was any relation to Jim Craig, the goalie for the US hockey team in the 1980 Olympics.

"That's my cousin!" I shrieked. "Remember after they beat the Russians and Jimmy, I call him Jimmy, looked up in the stands and you could tell he was saying, 'Where's my father? Where's my father?..? He was talking about my uncle!"

Had I known what Jim Craig's father's name was, I would have thrown that in to make it that much more believable. It's the little details that can make or break a good lie.

"Wow," said Mr Powers, somewhat star struck and obviously thrilled over his brush with history. He put his hand on my shoulder and then tussled the side of my head as if it were me who had not allowed any commie pucks into America's hockey net.

As soon as he rounded the corner my friend Mike and I could barely contain ourselves. From then on, as far as Mr Powers was concerned, I had a free pass at St Bernard's Catholic prep school and he was honored to have given it to me.

Like when he caught me and Dino smoking a joint out by the tennis courts. He told Dino to get the hell out of sight and keep his fucking mouth shut, and then brought me into his office. He gave me a cup of coffee and kept me for about an hour, hoping I would lose the effects of the pot so he could let me back out without any problems.

In return, I told him stories of my older cousin Jimmy and I as younger kids. The time I fell through the ice in a frozen pond and he carried me home. How he taught me to sail on his sunfish. When he used to make me get up early and shovel old peoples' sidewalks for free, sometimes without anybody even knowing who did it.

In the sports department of a Caldor's one day I found a small poster of the US Olympic hockey team. Mike and I autographed it with a few of the players' names, including-

Mr Powers, Thanks for looking out for my little cousin. He's not a rotten kid, he just smells like it. USA!

-Jim Craig

High school was a blast and I got all the ammunition I could want for debating religion. And then married somebody who refused to discuss religion with me. To this day I have no idea what her religious beliefs might have been.

I do know that she met a woman once who was a minister at a local Unitarian Universalist church. They started 'hanging out together' on Sunday mornings and Tuesday nights at 7:00. I was pretty sure she was cheating on me with religion but she refused to talk about it. The whole time we were married.

And one day, after we were divorced, we went out to lunch and when she started her car the radio was turned to gospel music and I still have no idea if she was just messing with me.

The Monstrosity at Mike's Chili

A staple of the Scottish Buddhist diet is the Monstrosity at Mike's Chili in Ballard. The Monstrosity is a grilled cheese sandwich with a hot dog on top, smothered in chili and beans with onion, cheese and jalapenos.

The Monstrosity is not on the menu and it probably never will be. The Monstrosity came to me in a dream, is best made by Steve on a weeknight, and was named by Mariah, who no longer works there. The price of a monstrosity varies according to who rings it up, as no one knows what one should cost. If you're not local to Seattle here's how to make it at home (though it's not as good)-

Homemade Monstrosity

Needed-
Butter
Onion
Garlic
2 pounds ground beef
1 can tomato paste
2 fresh tomatoes, diced
Green pepper, diced
Bag of kidney beans
Chili paste
Tabasco
Salt and pepper
Zantac
Hot dogs
Sourdough bread
Cheddar cheese
Jalapenos (pickled)

Soak the beans overnight. Canned beans are easier, but we're not animals, are we?

Prepare the Pot (see page 18)

Add the tomato paste, diced tomato, Tabasco, more garlic, another onion and some chili paste to the crock pot. Turn the pot to **Low**.

Brown and drain the beef, add to the pot. Cook for 4-6 hours.

About an hour before preparing the hot dogs and grilled cheese, add the kidney beans and take a double dose of Zantac.

Grill the hot dogs and cheese sandwiches. Butterfly the hot dogs, put on top of the sandwiches, cover with chili, and add freshly grated cheese, chopped onion and chopped jalapeno.

About a year after my wife and I moved to Seattle I got a shop and set up a boat business. Next door was a wood shop owned by a guy named Dave and I loved him immediately, like an older brother. The first place he took me to in Ballard was Mike's Chili Parlor and we went there every Saturday for lunch.

Dave's not around anymore but I still try to go there once a week. I have some chili and a couple beers and do the NY Times crossword puzzle like we used to do.

The second place Dave took me to in Ballard was just a standard beer and burgers kind of place and when we sat down at the bar, he made a production of ordering his beer. He was very adamant that his beer be served in a stem glass and even asked to look at what kind of glasses they had.

The busy bartender had little patience for Dave, but poured off half a beer in a wineglass while rolling her eyes. Dave downed his beer and began to teach me (his new little brother) an important lesson.

He looked around the bar and said, "If you ever have a problem with some asshole in a place like this, that beer glass ain't gonna help ya. Always drink your beer from a stem glass because if shit goes down you need a weapon. Just break off the base of your glass like this-" He mocked breaking off the base of his wineglass by hitting it on the bar on an angle, "and JAM IT INTO THEIR FUCKING THROAT LIKE THIS- AAAARRRGHH!!!!"

I suggested that maybe if he weren't drinking his beer out of a wineglass there would be less need to defend yourself, but he just tapped on the side of his head and told me I might use this information one day.

And he was right!

Our neighborhood was mostly small shops and a couple of abandoned houses. They were about to demolish one of these old houses so Dave and a couple other guys in the neighborhood went inside to see if there was anything still in there.

There wasn't much other than some golf clubs and some figurines, but Dave got excited and thought the figurines might actually be worth something. He went back to his shop to see if he could find some information in one of his books (he had a remarkable amount of books in his woodshop) and made a couple phone calls.

He came back a half hour later with a book in his hand all excited only to find Bill and Brian practicing their golf swings on rocks, now that the figurines were gone. "YOU WRECKED 'EM!!" Dave yelled.

"Now, Dave," Bill said, "there's no need for name calling."

And until his death, whenever Dave did something wrong we would yell- 'YOU RECTUM!'

Nobody's sure but we all think he never got the joke.

Suggested beverages- Mac and Jack's at Mike's, Redhook ESB at home.

Dave Dies

All growing up my family described me as moody. I was alternately full of energy or quiet and sulky. My cousin Mike was the same way. We were born ten days apart and were remarkably similar. When we were eighteen, I was in Texas and he was living with his parents. Everything seemed to be going well for him, and he had a cool girlfriend who cared about him. One morning, after driving around all night by himself, Mike came home at about six in the morning. He walked past his mother who was sitting in the kitchen without saying anything. He went upstairs and walked past his father who was shaving in the bathroom. He went into his room, pulled out a hunting shotgun and splattered his brains all over the wall.

I've never been able to forgive him for making his parents clean the inside of his face off the wall of his bedroom, but having come so close to pulling the trigger myself, I've forgiven him for wanting out.

Hardcore depression can creep up slowly, or it can hit you like an earthquake. My worst bout was sudden and long lasting. My best friend died without warning and it completely caught me off guard. The fact that he was a major part of my everyday life made it that much worse.

Dave was one of the greatest guys I've ever known. He had more friends than anyone I've ever met, and there was never a shortage of people who would stop by his shop or call him up just to see how he was doing. He was one of the first people I met when my wife and I moved to Seattle, and he became our surrogate West Coast family.

He made me a part of his daily routine and I loved him for it. After coffee and toast at Val's on Phinney, he would stop by my shop at about 9:15. He'd quiz me on what I'd be doing for the day and ask what I had done since seeing me the night before. He'd then go to his shop, which was right next door to mine. The next half hour to an hour was spent calling family and friends around the country. He'd get some work done, and then it was time for lunch. Mondays', Tuesdays', Thursdays' and Fridays' lunches were spent with various other groups of friends, but Wednesdays and Saturdays were mine. I had to share Wednesdays with Neil, but that was okay.

After lunch was more work, with maybe a break to come over to my shop to have a root beer and discuss some outrage he had heard on the radio. At the end of the day, we'd drink tea around his woodstove or beer in my shop. He and I would help each other out on projects we each did. Weekends were reserved for messing about on motorcycles and cars.

I was a little concerned one afternoon when I hadn't seen him, and got a call on my way home from Russ, one of his other best friends, who had known him since they were teenagers. "We lost him" was about all he was able to say. I drove back and parked in front of his shop and cried and yelled.

We had a party at his shop about a week later and the place was completely full of at least two hundred of his closest friends. Everybody seemed sad enough, but I couldn't help feeling like things wouldn't be alright. I wanted to shake people and yell at them- "He's gone! I don't want to hear another funny story, I want you to tell me what I'm gonna do without Dave!"

I felt abandoned and scared, and it affected me physically. I was dizzy because I could barely eat. I couldn't concentrate on my work and it suffered. My wife didn't know what to do with me. The most I could manage was to wait until it was time to go home, turn off my phone and lay on the couch and watch Comedy Central until I fell asleep. The morning was the worst time of day. I usually threw up within ten minutes of waking.

I remember thinking that everything was a hoax, including every time I previously thought I was happy. There was simply no way. And every happy person I saw had to be lying, or else they were too stupid to realize just how dreadful this existence really was.

After a month or two, Vanessa demanded I go with her to a psychiatrist. He was pretty quick to prescribe anti-depressants, and although I didn't see the point in them, I took them at my wife's insistence. It took a few weeks, but slowly I began to feel better. Then I started feeling a LOT better. Soon I was bouncing off my shop walls, coming up with all forms of new inventions.

An NFL player died in training camp of heat stroke and I sprang into action. I sent his family a note informing them how sad I was for their loss, and set out to make things right. I vowed to them that this would never again happen to another football player. I bought a professional football helmet and realized what everyone else had missed. There was no ventilation! I bored some holes in the top of it, and fabricated some carbon fiber inserts that would strengthen the openings and epoxied them in. I gave it some impact tests, and when I was certain I had found the answer, I drove out to the Seattle Seahawks training camp and tried to get a meeting with the Head Coach, Mike Holmgren. He wouldn't see me, even after several requests, including one in writing. At the close of camp, he was sitting outside signing autographs, but his assistants wouldn't let me get in line to show him my helmet. He watched me nervously as he signed hats and shirts.

I realized I needed an outlet, so I figured I'd take up a musical instrument. Naturally, I chose the bagpipe. Unfortunately, bagpipes were a lot more expensive than I thought they would be, so I decided to make my own. How hard could it be?

But my bagpipe wasn't gonna look like all those other common bagpipes already out there. My pipes were gonna be made of fiberglass and carbon fiber and not only would they look completely funky, they were gonna be louder and sound better than any other bagpipe ever made.

Since I now had all the energy in the world, it would not be a problem. Even though I was working sixty plus hours a week building and fixing boats, I had plenty of time at night since I had little need for sleep. I began experimenting with tone chambers, carbon fiber chanters, and home-made reeds. I found I was most productive when I was smoking lots of pot, drinking copious amounts of beer, and listening to the Butthole Surfers at full blast. My wife had a hard time believing this was acceptable behavior, so it was time for another visit to the head doctor.

She was concerned, of course, with the amount of alcohol I was able to consume. He asked how I behaved when I drank and she admitted that I was never abusive or mean in any way, and that it didn't really look like I was all that drunk. It just seemed wrong that I could have twelve or fifteen beers and then drink all the wine when the beer ran out.

He explained that I was bipolar and that while my drinking was certainly not a healthy way to live, it was my body's way of self-medicating my mania. The options, he explained, were to try some different meds or ride it out and see if I would level off. This manic depression, the ups and downs, he told us, would probably always be with me, and if she couldn't accept this, she should seriously consider leaving me.

I'm sure she felt a little cheated. Like buying a house and then ten years later finding out there's gonna be an international airport put in and the main runway abuts your backyard.

Sloppy Joes

When we first got married, Vanessa didn't eat red meat and I didn't eat fish. So we ate chicken. Lots and lots of chicken. Broiled and stir fried, mostly. And then one day I caught her eyeing my burger when we were out and I coaxed her into taking a bite. She became a very good cook and one of the best meals she made was Sloppy Joes. She didn't use a crock pot, but it was still one of my favorites.

Needed-
Butter
Onion
Garlic
2 pounds ground beef
1 green pepper
1 can tomato paste
Red wine vinegar
Sugar
Chili paste and/or Tabasco
Salt and pepper
Zantac
French bread

Prepare the Pot (see page 18)

Brown and drain the ground beef.

Add the beef, tomato paste, diced up green pepper, a splash of vinegar, some sugar, a little chili paste and/or Tabasco, and salt and pepper to the crock pot.

Turn the pot to **Low** and cook for 6 to 8 hours.

Take two Zantac and cut the bread. Sloppy Joes are best served open-faced.

Suggested beverages- A double hopped IPA, merlot.

NOTE- There are no chicken dishes in the Scottish Buddhist Cookbook.

Amber the Sea Gal

Amber was a Seattle Seahawks cheerleader. A Sea Gal.
She was, without a doubt, the most beautiful coordinated
dancer in the history of modern sports. Ever. I used to
joke around on the Seahawks.com message boards about
what a hard-on I had for her and all the things I'd like to
do to her, but it was all pretty harmless since I was married and she was Amber. Plus, I didn't actually own any
nipple clamps, anyway.

The 2001 Seattle Boat Show was coming up and I
decided to get a booth and see if I could land some good
jobs for the winter. I made a nice display and some new
Boat Fetish t-shirts to hand out. And I noticed on Amber's profile page that the SeaGals were available for
events. I called immediately and found that it was only
$175 for two hours! I told the events coordinator that it
had to be Amber, and after a short pause she said okay.
"Autographs are free!" she said. Whatever, I thought.

I didn't happen to mention to Vanessa that I
hired a cheerleader to come to my booth at the boat
show. She never got involved with my business at all, so I
reasoned she wouldn't want to feel like she had to stop by
and see how it was going. Besides, our marriage was on
the rocks and when I mentioned it months later, she just
rolled her eyes and made cruel jokes about me with her
friends.

The boat show was just four days after 9/11, and
there was hardly anybody there. I thought they might can-
cel the show, but instead, they made it free and hired a
bagpiper to play at noon. I walked out to the end of the
pier and, along with everybody else, cried a little when he
played Amazing Grace.

Amber showed up at one, and we practically had the whole boat show to ourselves. Since nobody in Seattle had any interest at that moment for a new swim platform or bow thruster, we just hung out and talked. It was a very insecure time for everybody, and the impact of 9/11 gave us the opportunity to really connect with each other. Everything we talked about had the backdrop of the shortness of life and how we all had to come together and protect each other. I desperately wanted to bury my face between her comforting breasts.

One of my new friends from the Seahawks.com message boards, Sean, said he was coming to meet Amber and I told him she was showing up at three, and he could come then and stay for ten minutes. And he was NOT allowed to call me Jayhawk, just in case she ever did read the message boards. In fact, I told him, pretend you don't even know me.

He showed up at ten to three wearing his Seahawks jersey and baseball cap, and carrying a football for her to sign. This was just about the time Sean lost his house and took up residence in a room of my shop, so I was pretty sure he wouldn't try fucking with me.

"Hi! I'm Your Daddy!" he told her with a big stupid smile, assuming she read the message boards and would recognize his user name.

"Um, I don't think so," she answered, looking to me for a little support as I stood up from my stool and leaned forward on the display.

I could tell he intended to stay for the whole ten minutes I promised him. He said something about dating a Miss Washington years ago and how incredibly gorgeous she was. "You're cute, but Mary Jo Pinkus was off the charts. Do you have an agent?"

"Alright, that's enough." I told him. "Other people want autographs, too, buddy."

He looked behind him and there was nobody there so he just mumbled "Jayhawk" and walked away.

I hadn't told anybody outside of the message boards that I had hired a Seagal because the last thing I wanted was a bunch of people milling around me and Amber. With Vanessa about to leave me I thought that having Amber to talk to would help.

When my two hours were up, I wasn't ready for it to end so I asked her if she wanted to walk around and check out the boats. She had just turned twenty-one a couple weeks earlier and grew up in Eastern Washington, and had never been on a boat before. We came to a 90' motor yacht and she was amazed. "You want to go in?" I asked her.

"You can go in?!?"

"Sure. It's for sale. Pretend we're married and we're looking for a new boat."

There was a broker couple and two crew members wearing matching red shirts. The male broker was quick to pour us each a glass of wine and had a big creepy smile that made Amber stick close to me. It was obvious she was a professional cheerleader, and whether they made a lot of money or not was irrelevant. The fact that she was with somebody like me obviously meant that I was rich.

We took our shoes off and they gave us the tour. Amber wanted to see the 'bedroom' first, because, "It's where we spend most of our time, right, Honey?"

I looked to make sure the male broker caught that and said, "That's right, Babe."

In the main stateroom, Amber jumped up on the bed and gave us all a pout when she couldn't stand up straight without hitting the headliner. They showed us the smaller staterooms for our guests, and then a berth in the back for the captain and his mate. "What about my chef?!?", she demanded.

As we were putting our shoes back on, she looked over to the boat next to us and said, "Ooh, I bet THEY have a hot tub!"

The next boat saw us coming and also gave us some wine. Amber had been paying attention on her first tour, and was ready with a couple of questions. "Is that African mahogany?" and "What kind of range do you get with this gal?"

And as happy as I was that Amber was getting a crash course in owning a yacht, I was ready for some food so I offered to buy her some lunch. "Duke's has the greatest crab chowder you'll ever have. Or we can go to Chandler's. Want some baked stuffed shrimp?"

"I saw a Hooters when I came in, can we go there?"

From the second we walked in the door, all the Hooters girls kept a steady eye on us. Our server was naturally very nice to me, but not so much to Amber. Our server, who we'll call Brandi, touched my shoulder and asked what I'd like to drink. Then she just looked at Amber and waited.

As she was walking away I remarked at how rude she was, but Amber just shrugged. "I'm used to it."

When Brandi came back with our drinks Amber said something nice about Brandi's body and then looked at me and said, "Isn't that right, Honey?" I completely agreed.

Brandi warmed up to Amber and a couple of the other Hooter girls found reasons to come over to talk to us. They mostly wanted to talk to Amber about being a professional cheerleader, but they were also curious about me. Amber could obviously have any man she wanted, so why was she with me?

"Well," I started when one of them flat out asked me what I did for a living, "I, uh, own a bagpipe factory."

"Wow, that's so cool!", one of them said. "There must be a lot of money in that."

"There sure is." Amber said. "That's why we came to the boat show. We need a bigger boat, right, Honey?"

When our food came out Amber's Buffalo Chicken Sandwich came with a side of baked beans. Amber grew up with her grandmother way out in the middle of Washington State and never went anywhere until she started competing in and winning beauty contests. Apparently, her grandmother never opened her up a can of baked beans.

"What are these?" she asked me, poking them with her fork.

"You've never had baked beans?" There was so much I needed to show her.

She carefully sampled them in the cutest, sexiest, most adorable way possible and I melted. I told Sean about it the next day and we joked at how shocked she must have been later to experience her first fart.

Baked Beans and Linguica

Linguica is a Portugese Sausage. It's awesome.

Needed-
Butter
Onions
Garlic
2 pounds dry kidney beans
Half a can of Guinness Draught
2 pounds linguica
½ pound brown sugar
Catsup
Mustard
Tabasco
Salt and pepper

In a large bowl, soak the beans in water and Guinness overnight.

In the morning, **Prepare the Pot** (see page 18)

Drain the beans, saving the liquid. Chop up and add the linquisa, second onion, brown sugar, half a bottle of catsup, a little mustard, a little Tabasco, and salt and pepper.

Add just enough liquid back into the pot to cover the beans. Turn pot to **Low**, and cook for 6 to 8 hours.

NOTE- You can also add half a can of pineapple chunks, if you have it.

Suggested beverage- Guinness Draught in a can.

'Look Alive, Leonard!'

With Vanessa gone, I had to learn how to cook for myself, which I did. I was also free to do whatever I wanted, which I also did. I expanded my boat business by doubling my staff and advertising. I built a loft in my shop and moved in so I wouldn't have to be bothered with driving home to sleep. I made crazy looking, fully functional Great Highland bagpipes.

And I drank. Waking up in a strange woman's house was a common occurrence. Waking up in the hospital only happened once but it was for something pretty stupid. Apparently (I was in full blackout, so I have no memory of this), I was in a bar and took offense to a hat some guy was wearing. He and his friends beat the crap out of me and I woke up in Harborview with a broken nose and the bottoms of both eye sockets blown out.

About a month or so before that, I tagged along with a bunch of new friends to a party after the bar had closed. I had been hitting on this cute blonde, but had to go to the bathroom or get a beer or something. When I got back, Leonard, the host, was crouched over talking to her. I yelled, "Look alive, Leonard!" and kicked him over, sending him crashing onto chairs and landing on the floor. He got up, said, "You shouldn't have done that, Jay" and bounced me face-first off the wall.

There was a definite pattern developing in which I put myself in situations that were ready-made for me to get my ass kicked. A couple of times, I even unwittingly involved my new friend Steven.

The first was when the longshoreman's union went on strike because they didn't want to upgrade their technology to become more efficient, as this might mean less jobs for their future sons and grandsons. I somehow convinced Steven this was an outrage and that we had to go down there and confront them.

I told him I would pick him up the next morning and went about making picket signs. We arrived down at their union hall and held up signs calling them commies, Mafioso, and un-American. One sign said, 'Fuck You! Get Back To Work, Traitors!'

I invited a reporter from the Seattle Times but he was clearly a union man and chose not to run a story.

When one of them almost hit us with his car, we decided to leave. On the drive back Steven said that was the stupidest thing he ever did, and he never mentioned it again.

The second time was when we went to a party in Tacoma and afterwards to a casino to watch some fights. I was pretty drunk and propped myself against a couple folding chairs on the back row of the main floor. Two couples came to sit and as one of the men started to take a seat in front of me, I looked over to Steven, gave him a 'check THIS out!' look and pulled the chair away. The guy went tumbling, everybody behind us started laughing, and Steven made a beeline for the other side of the box-ing ring.

The guy got up and it looked like he wanted to kill me, but he couldn't get a punch in 'cause I was laughing so hard, so he just yelled at me and his wife and the other couple convinced him to just find another place to sit. I offered to buy him a beer, but he told me to go fuck my mother. After the fights were over I found Steven as he was heading to his car and he gave me a ride back to Seat-tle, even though he didn't say two words to me the whole time.

Waking up in Harborview that one time with a swollen face was nowhere near the wake up call one might expect. Even looking in the hospital mirror didn't do much more than make me laugh at myself. My eyes were almost completely swollen shut and my face was purple. It took a few days before my eyes were opened enough to see that there was no white in them, only red. My teeth felt loose for several weeks and there is still some nerve damage on the left side of my face.

There are times when you can be so manic that the only way to come down is to be taken down violently. There's something about getting your face beaten in that's just a little bit satisfying. When you're depressed you think about killing yourself and when you're manic you need a reprieve. Death is forever but a good beating is just a much-needed break.

Pot Roast and Roast Pork

It amazed me when I first starting using the crock pot just how cheap and easy a good meal can be. They don't tell you this but you can make dinner for you and a friend, and then have great leftovers for a couple days after, for about twenty bucks.

Needed-
Butter
Onion
Garlic
3-4 pound roast
Baby potatoes
Baby carrots
Salt and pepper

Prepare the Pot (see page 18)

Salt and pepper the roast.

If you have time, it's best to cook each side on **High** for a half hour before adding the potatoes and carrots. Cook on **Low** for an additional 4 to 6 hours.

Or-

Just throw everything in the pot and cook on **Low** for 8 hours.

NOTE-
With a pot roast, a healthy splash of red wine is good.
With a roast pork, you can add an orange (poke it with a
fork first) and some cinnamon.

Suggested beverages- IPA, merlot.

Serve with chilled catsup.

The Ballad of Huggy Jesus

There's a new kind of feeling of
faith that's formin'
And Jesus don't care if you're
a Jew or a Mormon.
You could be from Texas or from ol' Bombay,
He's gonna love you 'cause He's just that way!

So step right up and grab a hug from God,
He's gonna hug you back twice as hard!
Huggy Jesus, He's our man!
He's got the whole world in His Hand!

Now you might think he was a son of a gun,
And you're right there, Charlie,
He was lots of fun!
He helped people out and He mighta been gay,
at least that's what I read just the other day!

So, come on people, you're mighty smart!
Just live and let live, it's not that hard!
Huggy Jesus got a plan!
If He can't do it, nobody can!

Huggy Jesus

I first met Sean online. We were both regular visitors to the Seattle Seahawks website and posted on their message boards. He had entered the discussion group in the most obnoxious way possible. If you're unfamiliar with message boards, here's how it works- when you enter a discussion group online you read what people are saying, look back at what has already been discussed, and try to get a sense of the place. And you understand that people have been talking for a while and have developed relationships.

What you don't do, is read one or two posts, decide everybody on the website is a total fucking idiot, and then make a long condescending argument as to why everybody should shut the hell up and just ask you directly if they have any questions about the topic at hand. And then, you don't sign off-

Your Daddy.

This was, of course, exactly what Sean did. We jumped all over him and he eventually changed his sign-off to Pops and became a favorite of the hundreds of visitors to the site. What he never lost, god bless him, was his sense of contribution to the future Super Bowl successes of the Seattle Seahawks.

"Don't you think Paul (Allen, the owner) and Holmgren (Mike, the coach) read these posts every day? Don't you think that if I walked up to Matt (Hasselbeck, the quarterback) and said 'Hi, I'm Pops!' he'd thank me for my tips on avoiding the pass rush? Dude! They read what we write! You don't think Paul Allen, one of the richest men in the world, doesn't know everything about me?! What if he thinks I might become a threat to him someday? You don't think he'd have me taken out? Come on!! You don't get THAT rich by not being paranoid! But I could walk up to his house right now and his security guards would recognize me, tell Paul Allen I'm there, and I'm in. That ain't no shit, Bubba! I was there when they were practicing on a field behind a school before the Kingdome was even built! He KNOWS that!!"

After several months of talking about the Seahawks, football, religion, Seattle, boats, etc., Sean asked me where I worked and showed up one day at my shop.

He amused me immediately. He was a character out of an Elmore Leonard novel. I had been under the impression he was a master machinist, so I was a little surprised at what he drove up in- an old black stinky dying mini-van with no windows in the back.

It didn't take long before he was telling me stories about strong-arming his way into a Mafia family in Miami, smuggling cocaine in from Columbia, blackmailing a female FBI agent (they're still fuming about that one, believe you me, Bub!), and armed robbery against a bank that screwed him out of some money in a house deal. They were great stories, and the level of truth didn't matter to me at all. And he gave some pot that he grew in his supposed vast underground grow operation.

He reminded me of my grandfather, Papa. Not everybody appreciated Papa like I did. I know he was an obnoxious pain in the ass, but I thought he was funny. I used to visit him at the nursing home every Sunday with a contraband Mars Bar and we'd watch a football game or a movie on TV. I'd wheel him out for a smoke and he'd tell me stories about World War Two and airplanes and ships.

When Papa was being admitted into the nursing home he underwent a mental evaluation and made a big impression on the resident psychiatrist. This doctor later told my parents that Papa was an amazing man. "It was an honor to meet him," he said. "I love World War Two history and to hear his experiences on the battlefield was fascinating! He described the feeling of being there so well, I felt like I was right next to him, under fire!"

My mother laughed. "He blew his knee out playing football in high school. They wouldn't let him in the Army. He stayed here and built airplane propellers. He just reads a lot."

I know Sean doesn't read books (he's too lazy) but I do know he watches a lot of movies. And this doesn't mean I doubt the legitimacy of what he's ever told me, because I know he's capable of anything. I just never cared if the stories he told me were true or not. Besides, I saw his underground grow room.

When Sean was evicted from his house I let him take up residence in a back office of my shop. He did a couple of mechanical jobs for me but it was immediately apparent why he couldn't hold a job as a machinist. He was much too intelligent to work for idiots.

I had little work for him so his day consisted mostly of waking up around eleven, hitting me up for a couple bucks (it cost me between five and twenty dollars a day to know him then), going to the food bank, and getting online on my shop computer to dispense his football wisdom.

And then one night I was having dinner with my ex-wife and we were talking about a girl I had starting seeing. It was soon after we had broken up and the divorce was still months away from being finalized so it was no surprise that she was a little brutal to Theresa. Vanessa had always had a disdain for women who have stuffed dolls and when I mentioned Theresa was a Christian, Vanessa said, "I bet she has a stuffed Jesus doll."

A light bulb exploded over my head! A Stuffed Goddamn Jesus Doll! Brilliant! What could be better than selling Jesus to the Christians? There's millions of them and there's already been two thousand years of pre-publicity! Everybody's heard of Jesus! This would be way easier than selling those stupid Cabbage Patch dolls or those crappy Beanie Babies!

I remembered Sean telling me that he'd once made a full-sized shark costume for Halloween (from the old Land Shark skit on Saturday Night Live), and that his mother used to make dolls. And he'd be the perfect frontman for it. A homeless guy who finds Jesus and wants to spread His love. This was gonna be great!

I told Sean about it the next day and he was all over it. We set to work sewing up some prototypes. I came up with Super Jesus, complete with a cape and a big JC on his chest and capable of leaping off His cuddly soft cross in a single bound. And Sean came up with the model we would use. His version won mostly because it looked like a little Charlie Manson with freaky blue eyes and a bunny nose, and I almost peed myself every time I looked at it. Huggy Jesus was born!

We had somebody make some dolls for us and we came up with a story about how Sean had found Jesus one day when he was at the lowest point of his life. We decided that he had gotten to the food bank after they had closed and, dejected, wandered around Ballard in the rain. He came upon a church and to his surprise, the door was unlocked. [At this point I wanted to say that he went in to steal something but Sean rejected that.] He walked toward the altar and fell to his knees. He began crying uncontrollably and begged God for help. After a couple minutes, he looked up and saw a vision of Jesus. Sean said 'Hi', but Jesus said nothing, for He had no mouth.

I had insisted from the start that Huggy Jesus would be mute. I did not want him to come with a message. I knew people would take it seriously and I did not want to send any messages about what Jesus would have to say to children. In part because I didn't think we should preach Christianity, but mostly because I knew that I could not be trusted to do it without having a lot of fun with it and ruining any chances of actually making any money off this.

Next came marketing. A friend of mine made us a website and I remember being a little surprised at the time that huggyjuses.com was still available. How could nobody else have thought of this? It was so obvious!

The billboards were great. Five of them around Seattle, with Huggy Jesus rising up out of the clouds, declaring HE IS COMING! Cost me five thousand dollars, but it was worth it. We got an 800 number and for every person who had to have one of these dolls there were two who thought we were gonna burn in hell for trying to profit off the Lord. It was great! The messages left on our answering machine were the best. Me and a couple friends would drink beer and sit around the answering machine laughing our asses off. Some people get very pissed off when you have a little fun with their savior, apparently.

We sold some dolls, got some press, and went through a few potential investors, all of whom tried to screw us. We finally got the owner of a pizza franchise (Sean's new boss, he was now delivering pizzas part time) to buy the licensing rights to Huggy Jesus. He spent over $70,000 and sold only a handful of dolls. Five thousand of them sat in a warehouse in Minnesota, despite his feeble attempts at marketing an established icon that's been around two whole millennia. He spent twenty thousand dollars trying to spam Christians but that didn't work. He paid $13,000 for a TV commercial we made (one of the funniest things I've ever seen) but only ran it locally and was put off when nobody in Seattle bought any. Several Christmas seasons have since passed with no action and it all became just a bad joke that was no longer funny. I'm pretty sure the remaining dolls were sold in lots for pennies on the dollar.

Huggy Jesus appeared once in a discount bin at a local novelty shop called Archie McPhee's and then, miraculously, He was featured on the website stupid.com until they were all gone. I've thought of resurrecting Him again, maybe as part of a line of religious figures- with a Huggy Buddha and a Huggy Mohammed, but so far have been unable to get any backers.

Lasagna

As with every recipe in this cookbook, you can pretty much play around with the ingredients based on what you like. If you like a really cheesy, fluffy lasagna, use a full 32 ounces of ricotta. If you like something a little flatter and saucier, use less. It's your lasagna. If you have a date with a vegetarian use artichokes instead of beef.

Needed-
Butter
Onion
Garlic
2 cans tomato paste
4 or 5 fresh tomatoes
1 pound ground beef
Ricotta cheese
Mozzarella cheese
Parmesan cheese
Cheddar cheese
Flat 'no boil' lasagna noodles
Oregano, if you have it
Zantac

Prepare the Pot (see page 18)

Keep the crock pot on **High** and add the tomato paste. Stir occasionally. After about an hour, dice up the tomatoes and add to the pot with a little oregano or basil. Mash well and cook for another 4 hours on **Low**. Brown the meat and drain off the grease. Add to the pot and mix well.

Remove the sauce and layer in the ingredients in the following order- sauce, noodles, cheese, sauce, noodles, cheese, sauce, noodles, cheese, sauce.

Cook on **Low** for 1 ½ hours (see note). Add lots of shredded cheddar and mozzarella and take two Zantac. Cook an additional half hour. Remove the lid, turn the pot off and let stand for about fifteen minutes.

NOTE- Do NOT overcook the lasagna! There is almost nothing worse in this stupid world than buying fresh goat cheese mozzarella from the Sunday Farmer's Market and having to throw the whole thing away because it's inedible.

Suggested beverages- Pale ale, merlot.

Cell Phone Vending Machines!

About the time we were negotiating the final details of the licensing deal for Huggy Jesus, tragedy struck. Sean lost his cell phone. He was beside himself. Suddenly, the whole world ground to a halt and nobody could do anything until he either found his phone or got it replaced. For two days, he was unbearable. Things were starting to happen, and the loss of his phone had rendered him impotent to utilize his superior business savvy and negotiating tactics to finesse the remaining details to his benefit.

Sean had been the face of and fake story behind Huggy Jesus, and just as we were finalizing the biggest contract of his life, he had an Idea.

I first heard of this Idea that Saturday morning when he called me at home from the shop. "Jay! Get down here! I have something for you! It's very important! I know you're probably hungover so I waited til seven to call you. Now get down here!"

He called me several more times until I finally arrived at about ten to find him outside waiting.

"Goddamnit! I told you this was important!"

"Sean..."

"Shut up and listen. I don't know why I'm even gonna offer this to you now, but I like you so I'm gonna let this go. But never do that again!"

He felt he could trust me ('Though I don't know why, after you made me sit here for three fucking hours when I have shit to do!") with this new Idea, but first there had to be some ground rules. "This idea is gonna require your full attention. No more of this half-assed shit!"

"Whole assed, got it."

"Shut up. You're gonna come work for me."

"No thanks."

"Will you please just shut up and listen?!?! I'm gonna make you rich, but you'll have to work for it. You will be my West Coast rep and I'll give you a portion of every unit you place. Are you ready to hear my idea or not?"

"Actually..."

"Cell Phone Vending Machines!!"

It was beautiful and so simple! He'd get a couple million dollars and set up all these vending machines around the world (starting in Hawaii) so people could have a cell phone for a couple of days until the battery runs out, when they could either re-up or drop it back in the machine for their deposit. AND, he would install surveillance cameras in the machines and sell all the information and video to the FBI, because so many of his customers would obviously be using his phones for illicit purposes.

He laid out his plan in detail. Investment opportunity, employee benefits and profit sharing, even the huge cylindrical building with thousands of video monitors and a guy sitting on a chair at the end of a long boom that he controls to zip around and watch all the people buying phones and walking past his machines. This man would be wired into the FBI, of course. And he told me everything he was going to do with his newfound wealth.

"The first thing I'm gonna do is buy the Seahawks. Paul's a great owner, don't get me wrong, but I'm gonna be more active. I'm gonna buy all the players beach houses in the Bahamas as incentives to play better, maybe then Springs will hold onto the fucking ball. I'm gonna rearrange the entire secondary, bring in some new blood. And

Special Teams! The coach, what's his name? He's gotta go."

"Rodriguez. They fired him. It was in the paper this morning."

He swept his arms out and had a very self-satisfied look, as if he had orchestrated the entire event without even trying.

He basked in his glory for a moment and then asked me, "How much do you think it'll cost to get tinting in the owner's box?" He grabbed the phone book and looked up window tinters. "This one looks good."

"When you're the owner of the Seahawks, I don't think you'll have to shop around for tinting. I think all you'll have to do is tell somebody you want it and that's it."

"You're probably right." He sat down for the first time and was quiet. He looked over at the clock and jumped up. "Shit! I'm late. I have to go deliver pizzas!"

He was very busy for the next two weeks putting his plan into action. His un-submitted proposal to the director of the FBI and a copy of his sent letter to Ted Turner (the obvious choice to fund such a project) are two of my prized possessions.

He somehow talked a friend of his who owned a restaurant into giving him $20,000 by leveraging his future earnings to Huggy Jesus. Which, in retrospect wasn't such a bad idea. Unless you were the restaurant-owning friend, of course.

Sean now had twenty grand at his disposal, and he was gonna do this right. He already had everything written down and drawn up, and he carried his Plan and schematics with him wherever he went. He told every single person he met ("You can never tell who's got money just by looking at them! Ever see a picture of Howard Hughes before he died?") that he had something in his briefcase that was gonna make him rich beyond words, and if they wanted in they better get together as much money as possible, and get it quick. Sell their house if they have to, just get it together before somebody else does or they're gonna hate themselves for the rest of their lives. He couldn't divulge what the Idea was, though. They would just have to trust him.

It was suddenly very important that Sean now carry himself with a new air of dignity. Nobody was going to throw hundreds of thousands of dollars at him if he looked like just another worker bee, and to watch him go through this total reformation was a fascinating thing to behold.

In addition to dying his hair black and getting a professional to clean his nails, he invested in a new wardrobe. Namely, an official Seattle Seahawks football jersey (number 8, with Hasselbeck on the back), a matching nylon windbreaker/pants ensemble, and of course, a golf cap. A quick look at him would tell any investor with half a brain what Sean's noble yet simple intentions were- to own the Seahawks and craft multi-million dollar deals over a leisurely eighteen holes.

The next problem to address was his car. A stinky noisy unreliable old mini-van with no windows in the back was certainly not befitting to his new image. About six months previous I traded my shop van for a BMW 528I that needed a new motor. Sean took the job of swapping out the motor but never quite got around to finishing it, so it sat in my shop. I couldn't sell it until it was running so I resigned myself to bringing it to somebody else to finish it up when he came out to a boat I was working on one day and threw $500 at me.

"Jay, I'm gonna do you a favor, even though you've been a real dick lately," he told me in front of my customer. "I'm gonna buy the Beamer from you for $2,000, but you gotta paint it black with NO RUNS! I want your best paint job or it's no deal! I'll pay for the paint and labor it takes one of your guys to prep it out, you just spray it."

He gave me a deadline to have it done ("One week!" "No way." "Okay, next month." "Maybe." "Deal!") and then spent the next two weeks looking at the car, no doubt imagining himself driving around in it with its bitching new paint job, black with gold metallic ("I saw that once on a car in Miami. Very classy!")

It had been less than a week since he got the money but he'd been working very hard. Or at least Thinking very hard. It was time for a vacation. Fortunately, it was the time of the year the NFL held its Pro Bowl. In Hawaii, no less! He could take a break AND do some work. He would scout out their international airport ("Lot's of Asian's go through there. Asians LOVE cell phones!"), get in some golf ("Bet you a thousand dollars I get my big investor before the ninth hole!"), and introduce himself to his future employees, the Seattle Seahawks. "Bet you another thousand me and Paul figure out a deal that gives me the Hawks in trade for a little bit of SellFonz (or whatever he was calling it). It's just gotta be done in a way that he doesn't lose face."

When he got back from Hawaii, he didn't offer too many details. No, there were no Big Deals struck on the golf course, but he did sit next to a very attractive tennis player on the shuttle back to the airport. He showed me the picture he took of her with his fancy new cell phone and it was, indeed, Serena Williams. "Is she any good?", he asked me.

About a week later he was at the boatyard with his new personal assistant, Jessica. This was his third personal assistant since he got back. The first was his sister, who he had to fire 'cause she was a stupid bitch. The second couldn't keep up with him as he dictated his thoughts on the golf course. And now, Jessica. She is surprisingly hot. Whatever he said to her while she was dying his hair a couple weeks earlier, she obviously bought.

Several years ago Sean had acquired an old wooden boat at auction for $5. When he got evicted from his house he had the boat, which had been in his driveway, moved over to the boatyard where I did most of my work.

"There's my boat I was telling you about! A '59 Chris Craft Constellation! She's a classic! I'm living on it to save money. I'm trying to spend my resources wisely. That's what you do."

Jessica looked confused. "Where?"

"Right there!" Sean said, pointing to several different colored tarps, weather-worn and covering what could have been a boat. Or a bus. Or several cords of firewood. "I'm restoring it! I'm gonna bring it down to Mexico and charter it out for fishing trips! I've got it all set up! They're waiting for me down in Xiajautinau! Wanna go?"

Corn Chowder

Needed-
Butter
Onion
Garlic
Package of frozen corn
Can of creamed corn
3 potatoes
2 cups milk
Flour
Precooked bacon
Shredded cheddar cheese
Salt and pepper

Prepare the Pot (see page 18)

Dice the potatoes and bacon, mix about three tablespoons of flour into the milk, and combine all ingredients into the crock pot. Turn to Low and cook for 6-8 hours.

NOTE- If you're looking to get laid, add some chilled crab on top when served.

Suggested beverages- Pale ale, white wine, champagne for the ladies.

Proposal to the Director of the FBI
From Sean Patrick XXXXXXXXX

Dear Director,

I am currently assembling a small company to design, build, place and service vending machines that will dispense and provide immediate access to working cell phones billed to my customers credit or debit cards.

My target customers will be people traveling in and out of airports, train stations, bus stations, shopping malls, hotels and motels who are in need of uncomplicated immediate access to cell phone communication on a rental basis with no commitment. I am even considering a vending machine that accepts a ten-dollar bill for ten minutes of unrestricted phone calling. That "10/10" machine will obviously get abused by people the less than good intentions. For the protection of my investment in cash-and-carry phones with no hard reason to return these 10/10 phones back to the vending machines, I will build a real time video monitoring system into my design. These phones will also sound an alarm in the phone after the ten minutes of cell time are up or the phone is taken more than 100 feet from the vending machine. This activity will be considered theft and will trigger a GPS device for aid in the recovery of my stolen property. The thief will not know this. Finding the thief will be easy but perhaps it might be an advantage to the FBI to see what some of these thieves are up to besides stealing my phones. I will report every theft of a phone to whatever authority you choose with a picture of the thief. You will have an arrestable offense to pursue when and if you choose to make use of that circumstance. I will not care about the actual return of this phone but it will be an excellent reason to start an investigation of a person of interest.

This business could be an obvious thorn in the peace and tranquility of our world from time to time so I would like to make the Federal Bureau of Investigation an offer I am hoping you will consider expediently. I believe that allowing the FBI in on the 'ground floor' as I am building this company could be enormously beneficial to both myself and your organization.

In short, I am willing to add design and function that would benefit the FBI or local law enforcement to my vending machines and/or cell phones, which are called 'DAYFONZ'. My vending machines will look like a refridgerator-sized cell phone. At this time, besides the fact that I have designed into the concept a 24/7 video surveillance from inside the machines to help protect them from theft and to have photographic documentation of my transactions with my customers, I will be considering other methods of documenting my encounters and transactions with my customers. The video camera is triggered by a proximity sensor, so even anyone 'casing' my machine will also be documented. There could be obvious benefits to the FBI and other law enforcement to have unrestricted access to the information generated from the use of my telephones and vending machines and surveillance I will own as my company does its business from day to day in the highest traffic areas on our planet.

Today is Sunday the 25th of January, 2004. I intend to have a working, beautifully painted and 'finished on the outside full-size mock-up' of my vending machine by the end of February, 2004. That is one month away. I already have a location, 3439 16th Ave W in Seattle to build the 'mock-up demonstrator' and the materials and the funding ($20,000) to do the fiberglass shell with 'some' functionality to help sell my concept to future partners. I am going to immediately pursue interested investors with access to funding to help start growing my company as fast as humanly possible as soon as I have completed building a couple of acceptable mock-up vending machines to aid in demonstrations to gain funding.

What I need from you... or more to the point what I am proposing is that you do a quick study of this proposal and get back to me before other investors are on board. If you consider helping fund my company and show an interest in what I am proposing, I will, for a short period of time, be in position to offer you and your organization true exclusivity. I will slow my timing down to accommodate your timing needs as long as my estimated income and arrival in my checking account of said income is not suffering from any delays caused by needs of yours to participate in the endeavor... meaning... you will be required to offer a substantial deposit of $250,000 deposited directly into my personal checking account to put this on hold for the time it takes to accommodate your needs. There will be a reasonable limit to the time I will allow your needs to be met. Within no longer than one calendar year from the time I have delivered this proposal to your Seattle office, which will be Monday the 26th of January, 2004, I will at that time proceed on my own. I will immediately start pursuing other funding without being able to guarantee the FBI anything.

Sincerely,

Sean XXXXXXXXX, XXXXX Communications

Potatoes Au Gratin

Needed-
Butter
2 onions
Garlic
About 8 potatoes
Can of Spam
Lots of shredded cheddar and parmesan cheese
2 cups milk
Flour
Salt and pepper

Prepare the Pot (see page 18)

Cut the potatoes and Spam into cubes, chop up the second onion, and combine with milk, cheese, 2 tablespoons of flour, and salt and pepper. Turn crock pot to **Low** and cook for 6 to 8 hours.

A half hour before serving, add a layer of parmesan cheese to top.

Suggested beverages- Guinness Draught (the one in the can).

August 27th, 2004
Ted Turner III
Turner Enterprises / Ted Turner Pictures
133 Lucky Street NW
Atlanta, Georgia, 30303

Dear Sir,

Ted, and I hope I may have the privilege to call
you Ted, it is my sincerest desire that you can take time
from your demanding schedule and valuable attention to
read this letter. My name is Sean XXXXXXXX. I am a
machinist and investor of sorts. Perhaps, if you have visit-
ed Bill Gates' house in Medina, you have seen some of my
work. If you looked out of any of his windows you have. I
designed, manufactured and installed most of the trick
computerized window treatments throughout his residence. I was especially pleased with the Venetian blinds
with the solid brass head rails in his study.

The real reason for this letter is to inform you that
I have chosen you as the second person with enough resources to know that the golden goose is alive and well
and living in Seattle, Washington. No, I am not crazy or
some kind of whacko. I have chosen you because of what
I have seen of your life. It started with letting your news-
casters wear paper bags on their heads in the mid-
seventies. Your sailing was also very impressive. Having
crewed as foredeck for a factory boat 'Clark Sailboat
Company' up here in Washington I know how hard it is
to what you did in winning the America's Cup races. I'm
sure you are a busy man so I will get straight to the point.

I saw your interview on Charlie Rose's show a few
weeks ago and I made up my mind that if my primary
choice to invest in my latest invention didn't come
through in a timely manner that I would offer you a shot.

Well, my retired friend Ed, who is wealthy by most Seattle standards, has had untimely family problems recently and I have given him more than ample time to work them out. Now I am in a position to trot out the aforementioned goose for you to have a gander at. One thing that struck me about your interview with Charlie was that you would probably like to get back on top of the media/business world if only to show those Disney and Time-Warner chumps that they are not now, nor have they ever been ALL THAT. I would like nothing better to, and I believe I can, offer you the opportunity to do just that.

My latest invention is not a better potato peeler. At times I wish it was. It is more an invention of a system and how to apply it than any one thing or widget. This new way of doing business will, with no doubt in my mind or any fiber of my being, tap into a previously ignored market to the tune of many tens of billions, if not hundreds of billions of dollars within the next ten years. Do you remember your response to Charlie's question, "How you made it?" And you replied "I have the ability to see a little further over the horizon." I can't say that I have you history of savvy. But I can say that we share a similar view of the horizon. Except for the part when one of my heroes abandons what he is best at and sells buffalo burgers. Sorry. It just took me totally by surprise to see one of the planets best media minds going in that direction.

My "system" is more profitable than billboards, has a co-efficient cost to revenue that pales any form of television or publishing. I have been working 16 hours a day on this idea for eight months. It got its birth the day I lost my cell phone one day before some very important contract signings with the Envision 'George Foreman Grill' people licensing another invention of mine, a children's plush doll, 'Huggy Jesus'. That mishap set in motion a panic and response to not being able to replace my telephone soon enough facing imminent and critical communications concerning signing some important documents. I solved that problem and in the process created a new way to market similar 'high ticket' products, like cell phones, as well as putting my system in a position to benefit in many other ways, including selling advertising, in which you are an expert.

Because of the potential for a man with your resources to take my system to market I must insist on a non-disclosure agreement before I can be more specific about the details of how I designed this golden goose. I would be satisfied from you to non-disclosure, pending a written one, in person on the phone to achieve that end. This is an offer to negotiate a partnership using my invention and some of your money. My goal is to double your wealth, if it is true that you have 10 billion give or take, and to put me in the same category within possibly as short as five years. This business will not be susceptible to the stock or any other type of market. Your requirement is to buy in with 10 to 20 million dollars, the variable being how fast we want to win the lion's share of this new market, pick the cherries and organize the licensing of the apples. Your financial participation will reflect on how much I will be willing to offer as reward for your interest. A certain amount of manufacture is involved. Not being constrained by time-consuming meetings or permission from any other authority, I have been able to move rapidly to arrive at this point. The details large and small have already been studied and worked out. Prototyping, R&D and models manufacture to market have been accomplished. I already have a complete team in place ready to manufacture, place and market my system.

We are ready to make this goose fly. I project going into the marketplace within three months of funding. All the technical, logistical and financial model data is available for your review. If this proposal, as vague as it is, sounds interesting you must indicate that desire to me in person or in the form of a person-to-person telephone call within one week of the receipt of this letter. I will not make this offer to any other party for that period of time. If I get a positive response to this offer you will need to schedule one day in Seattle within two weeks after signing the contract at your expense. If you choose to participate I want to start manufacturing no later than Jan 1, 2005. We should be able to work the details of this proposed arrangement in the form of an LLC before then. I know this is a bit to absorb from an unsolicited offer. I am quite serious and believe wholly in what I have and what I have proposed.

Take another chance, Ted. You don't get to see that many golden geese in one lifetime.

Phone 24/7- 206-423-XXX

Sincerely,

Sean XXXXXXXXX, owner

Mr Pallet

There's a big Polish asshole out there named Mr Pallet who defecates in buckets.

Mr Pallet moved into a vacant lot next to the boat business I had by Fisherman's Terminal in Seattle. He was somehow able to rent the small patch of dirt next to me and I was told by his property manager that it was just for pallet storage. At first he seemed a little innocuous, but within two weeks he was the bane of my existence.

In less than a month he had moved in at least ten shitty broken cars and a trailer to live in. There was no electricity and no water, so being the resourceful piece of shit that he is, he got a loud gas-powered generator and a couple of five gallon plastic pails to crap in.

There seemed to be nothing that Mr Pallet would pass by on the side of the road. His main focus, of course, was broken pallets that he would bring back, refurbish, and sell for four dollars a pop. But if there was a half a bike, part of a chair, a sofa that was missing its upholstery, a dead battery, a piece of garden hose, a sign, a tricycle missing the front wheel, some bottles, an oar, an old tarp or a piece of metal, he would throw it in the back of his truck and unload it all to the delight of his partner in grime, Mrs Pallet.

I would have customers drop off their boats and be greeted by Mr Pallet, shirtless but with a kidney belt, drinking beers at ten am, yelling 'Woo Hoo! It's my birthday!' regardless of what day of the year it was. Sometimes he would hire a transient who would be walking by (we were right next to a train refueling station and there were plenty of men fresh off the rails) and the two of them would cut slats and affix them to pallets for an hour or two, and then start drinking. And asking my customers about the cars they drove and commenting on the boats they brought me.

I first went to the property manager, a guy named 'Harry' who manages property all around Ballard who told me, pretty much, to go fuck myself and mind my own business. So I brought in the Health Department. And the Fire Department. And Zoning.

Over the course of the next two months Mr Pallet would grow very upset with me. I took great pleasure in calling in the Health Inspector, who would arrive with a police escort and Animal Control. And several times I brought in the Fire Inspector, who was very concerned with the thousands of sticks of kindling masquerading as usable pallet parts.

One day I told him to move his truck because it was blocking my parking area. He told me it would be a little while because he was unloading a bunch of crap and would I mind waiting? Actually, I DID mind waiting and if he didn't move that piece of shit truck right now I was gonna slash his fucking tires. He got all pissed off and got in his truck and sped off. About halfway down the block he turned around and came racing towards me and swerved away just before running me over. But as he passed I took a swipe at his mirror and knocked it off. There was more yelling and Mrs Pallet called the cops. When the police arrived he told them I attacked his truck and I told them he tried to run me down and as I jumped out of the way, his truck hit my fist. The cops seemed to think it was all pretty funny and had no interest in getting either of us to press charges.

Finally, after several more visits from the City of Seattle's various departments, Mr Pallet and the property owner had amassed $22,000 worth of violations. The last time they showed up was to remove him and he did not go peacefully. He spent four or five days in jail and I thought it would be an opportune time to get his crap out of there. All of it.

I called Harry and told him that the time had come to bring in some dump trucks and some heavy machinery 'cause if Mr Pallet got out of jail and came back to this shit hole I was gonna FREAK OUT! I told Mrs Pallet that the trucks were coming and suggested she get what she wanted and get the hell out of there and quick. She took the trailer and that was the last I ever saw of her.

After two days of no action I called Harry and suggested that the next time he's on the viaduct coming back from Fisherman's Terminal he look over to his right and let me know if the banner I put up was legible enough, or should I make a bigger one? It said-

THIS PIECE OF SHIT MANAGED BY HARRY BAWLEY OF BAWLEY REALTY

The next day a backhoe and a couple dump trucks arrived and began smashing up Mr Pallet's stuff, including a 30' boat and several cars and trucks, and hauling it away. I got a twelve-pack, grabbed a pellet rifle, and spent the day shooting at all the rats that came scurrying out of his garbage pile.

If he ever went back there after getting out of jail, it wasn't while I was around. I do, however, see him on occasion now around Ballard. He'll yell at me and tell me he's gonna ruin me and I'll suggest he go shit in a bucket.

Ravioli (or Linguini) with Meatballs

Needed-
Butter
2 onions
Garlic
2 cans tomato paste
4 large fresh tomatoes
2 pounds ground beef
2 eggs
2 pieces of bread
Milk
Salt and pepper
Oregano, if you have it
Zantac
Ravioli (or linguini)
Rolls
Parmesan cheese

Prepare the Pot (see page 18)

Keep the crock pot on **High** and add the tomato paste. Stir occasionally. After an hour, dice up the tomatoes and add to the pot with a little oregano. Turn to **Low**.

In a large bowl, pour just enough milk on the bread to let it soak up. Add the ground beef, more onion and garlic, eggs, more green spices, and salt and pepper. Mash well, form into little meatballs and submerge in the sauce. Cook on **Low** for another 6 hours, skimming off the grease every so often. Take a double dose of Zantac.

Suggested beverages- IPA, merlot.

Sunshine

After my divorce I lived in my shop and spent most of my spare time chasing all the cute girls who wear the short dresses. But at a certain point I thought it would be a better idea to live among other people and try to settle down a little bit. So I found a place on CraigsList that sounded pretty good. An old Zen center in Ballard (my favorite Seattle neighborhood), 100 years old, a bunch of fruit trees, right behind the Ballard Market (open 24 hours), a variety of roommates...

I walked up on the porch and through the kitchen window saw everybody sitting around a table and much to my delight, they were mostly very cute and very youngish. 'I'll take it!', I thought before I even walked in the door.

And when I did walk in, I was met with Miranda (a hippie chick with dreds, but otherwise very pretty), Brooke (a member of suicidegirls.com, a goth/punk/soft-porn site for mostly bi-curious cute, but dangerously young girls), Heather (another suicide girl), a dude named John, and...

Sunshine.

Just sitting there at the table in a rare case of inertia. Totally inappropriate. The way I should have met her was in a field of poppies or at a demolition derby. Stuck up a tree, backing into my car, hitting me in the head with a boomerang, or trying to sell me Tibetan witchcraft. Instead, I met her sitting down.

"What's you favorite color?" she asked me. Dark green, I guessed. "Okay," she said, and I was in.

I'd never say this to her face, but the truth is I fell in love with her immediately. I'm sure if she knew it, but she was always kind enough not to toy with me. I pictured her as my adorable little prize in a world where hardly anybody ever gets what they want.

She had a boyfriend, but he was almost never around. And a pathetic story about an idiot ex-husband, who I swore I would punch in the throat if I ever met him.

Matthew, the boyfriend, was young, funny, good looking and drove a motorcycle. But he was also extremely vain and a little too eager to go out with his buddies, even at the expense of his beautiful girlfriend. I wanted to throttle him.

"What's the matter with you?", I asked him one day. "Laura (the name everybody else used for her) is one of the greatest people I've ever met. She's a peach and you have no idea what you have. You're an idiot."

And what she told me about her foray into marriage baffled me.

The ex-husband confessed on their wedding day to sleeping with a girl he had just met. A girl he had actually brought to their wedding and introduced to his new wife at the reception. She looked unwashed and smelled like cigarettes. Sunshine told me that she had looked forward to a life of domestic bliss and I was filled with jealousy. She had divorced him immediately, of course.

Sunshine grew up in a Mormon family, but it didn't take. She was the third of five children and according to her parents, will be the only one who will not be joining them in whatever, exactly, they knew was awaiting them in the next life.

She couldn't be too specific about all the details I desperately wanted to hear. Had she been a better Mormon daughter she would have gotten further into the inner sanctum of one of the freakiest of the freaky religions. But all she could provide were stories about disappointed parents who pleaded with her to stop thinking for herself and devote her life to the Heavenly Father so she could score her own planet when she died.

Her photo album had two of the greatest pictures I've ever seen, but when she first showed them to me, she had no idea they were funny.

One was a picture of her brother and his friend dressed up on Halloween. They wore white shirts, black ties and black pants. But they also had on funny hats. I asked her what they were supposed to be. "They're Mormons with funny hats," she told me, as if addressing an imbecile.

The second was a picture of her and a male friend saying goodbye at an airport as he was setting off on his 'mission'. I asked her why they were gathered in close for a picture, as if giving each other a farewell hug, yet keeping a good six-inch distance. They were giving each other an air hug.

I had to know what was up with THAT, but she just looked at me again like I was an idiot and slowly explained to me that for the couple of months before heading out on their 'work', missionaries were not allowed to have any physical contact with members of the opposite sex.

The little tidbits she allowed me were nowhere near what I craved but they were more than enough to explain why she fled that environment, became a Jack Mormon (their phrase for sheep that stray) and decided to marry somebody who was completely unworthy of her.

We had dinner one night and decided on getting tattoos the next day. She had already drawn up some flowers and imagined, eventually, twelve different floral tats on various parts of her body. "Even when I'm eighty

I'll still appreciate them," she said. "All old ladies love hibiscus and lilies."

The first would be a crocus (or something) on her left breast. She drew a beautiful flower, wrapping around a one inch circle that would be her nipple.

She told me that she had mentioned to her parents a week earlier that she was considering some tattoos. Even though her soul was already lost, they still protested. "You can't deface your skin! Heavenly Father forbids it!", her father pleaded with her.

"But Jessica (her older sister and a good Mormon) got a tattoo on her ankle," she pointed out.

"That's different. She's letting it fade," he told her in all seriousness.

I toyed around with a few ideas for my tattoo. I drew a large asterisk and filled it in with plaid. "It's a Scottish Asshole!", I suggested, remembering something from Kurt Vonnegut about an asterisk looking something like an asshole.

I drew a quick picture of Saint Patrick and offered, "Hey look! It's an Irish Asshole!"

Sunshine looked at me, expressionless, and I hung my head. "Oh god, I'm the only one who thinks I'm funny."

She gave me a belated belly laugh and a heartfelt smile that assured me she would always be my friend. "I'm so glad you moved in here, Jay," she told me. It was one of the nicest things anybody's ever said to me.

Beef Stew

The whole reason I first got a crock pot was because I thought I could have a constant pot of food, always ready to eat. I would keep the pot perpetually on and add to it as it got down. One day I'd stop and get a couple potatoes, the next day, some more beef. I hate shopping but if all I had to pick up was an onion, some garlic, maybe a bag of frozen corn, it wouldn't be so bad.

I did this for about a week and I was proud of myself. I bragged about it to my mother, my ex-wife, a female friend, and a couple male friends. All the guys thought I was pretty smart. Mom, Vanessa and Valerie, however, told me I was an idiot. They acted like I was brewing up some kind of bacterial soup that would kill me and infected all the other live-aboards in the marina.

So here's my recipe for beef stew. If you're a dude, know that you can keep this stew going indefinitely (you will have to add water occasionally). If you're a female, just save it, okay. Besides, this book isn't meant for you.

Needed-
Butter
Onions
Garlic
Stew meat
Potatoes
Frozen corn
Flour
Bottle of Guinness
Salt and pepper

Prepare the Pot (see page 18)

Cut up the meat into one inch pieces and add to the pot. Leave on **High** and cook for about an hour. Flip the meat and cook for another hour.

Cut up the potatoes and more onion, and add to the crock pot with corn, a little flour, Guinness, a glass of water, salt and pepper. Turn pot to **Low**.

Suggested beverage- Guinness.

Limited Term Bridget

After a few weeks of dating and monogamy, Bridget demanded to know Where We Were Going. "I'm gonna be forty in a few years. I'm no spring chicken anymore, Skirt." What she wanted, I suspected, was some idea of how long she could expect we'd be together. I thought it an odd request at first, but I played along anyway.

With ten years of marriage and a successful divorce under my belt, it made sense that people should enter into relationships without the stress of when it might end. Why not agree, from the onset, when it's over?

I suggested we set a date. Let's have a regular relationship, monogamous and all that, and in a couple of months, say July Fourth weekend, it's over and we go our separate ways...? That way, we could just enjoy our time together and there would be no hard feelings when it was over. A Limited Term Relationship.

In fact, I explained, maybe if all marriages were Limited Term, we wouldn't have any need for divorce. Couples could enter into a Three, Five, or for the more adventurous, Ten Year Limited Commitment. They would put up a deposit and when their time is up they can either use that money for the legal costs of a divorce, or re-up for another term. If they separate, both parties divvy up any crap they might have accumulated together and they move on. And if either party bails early, they get nothing. It's perfect!

Fourth of July weekend gave us a couple of months, which I thought was more than enough time to be with someone who referred to me only as 'Skirt'. I was prepared for a relaxing, stress-free, eight-week fling that might even end in fireworks. What I got, however, was a bitter, sarcastic, mean-spirited two month long re-enforcement of my unfailing ineptitude in dealing with the opposite sex.

We had first in a bar and she initially refused to go out (or home) with me because of the kilt. "Put on some pants and take me to dinner, Skirt."

I suggested we go back to her place and I'd gladly take off my kilt. "It's a skirt," she countered, "and you gotta buy me dinner first."

Bridget is Irish and enjoys a good pint. I ran into her several times over the course of a few weeks at Mulleady's, which was convenient to both my shop and her apartment.

She gave in and we started dating. Things were good for a while but I was increasingly uncomfortable with the rigors of being in a relationship and I felt like at any time it would get ugly because I was nowhere near ready to be anybody's boyfriend.

One day in late June we were dogsitting Steven's dog, GOD, at his house while he was away. That Sunday morning Bridget suggested we go up to her uncle's cabin in the Cascades for a few days.

"What, next weekend?" I asked.

"Whenever...", she said, staring at me.

I braced myself for some unpleasantness and realized that instead of a little morning sex, I was about to get into an argument that would no doubt lead to her getting dressed and storming out. And then her calling me up a couple times in the afternoon to yell at me.

"Okay. Since the Fourth of July falls on a Friday, how about we just extend through the weekend," I offered, preemptively. "Yeah. We could spend our last weekend up in the mountains at you're uncle's place. That would be nice."

"You're not serious."

"We agreed," I said defensively. "We discussed this right from the beginning. We'd have some fun and enjoy each other's company, and then..."

"I didn't think you meant it! I thought you were just being an asshole!"

We went to her uncle's cabin in the mountains for a few days. We bought a bunch of wine and beer and barely made it through the logging roads up to the cabin in my convertible. We had some snacks, but since there was no electricity we knew we wouldn't be cooking so we didn't bother bringing more than cheese and crackers, a little jerky, some pot, and lots of alcohol. By the second day we were drunk, dehydrated and hungry. But at least we had plenty of beer and wine.

I don't remember much about the weekend, but when I got home I had a notebook full of ramblings all about my new religion- Scottish Buddhism. The only things worth saving, though, were the Eleven Demandments of Scottish Buddhism and the basis for a Limited Term Contract. Everything else was incoherent or just plain stupid.

Bridget's patience was running low and she didn't seem to get Scottish Buddhism or even care that she was witness to the formation of a system of beliefs that would likely guide humanity through its next, and possibly final, phase. I explained to her that this was bigger than the both of us. Still she was unimpressed and we stopped seeing each other when we got back.

But every religion has to start somewhere and just because the one with Jesus in it has been around for two thousand years doesn't make it any better than mine, right? The Jews have been around a lot longer but all that means is that they haven't evolved. Islam is Islam, Hindus still worship cows, and all the traditional Buddhist religions exist solely to push all forms of shiny drivel like eternal life, karma and enlightenment. I could do way better.

I never told anybody this, but when I was a kid I honestly thought I was the Second Coming of Christ. It felt like the world was all set up for me and that when I was older, say, in my thirties, all would be revealed. I knew enough to keep it to myself and it never occurred to me that anybody else might ever feel that way. Why would they? I was New Jesus, not them.

There were no coincidences in my world. Everything was a sign of my looming Revelation. And of course the next JC would also be a JC. The Second Coming was not gonna be run by some kid named Bobby, I knew that much.

Like so many others who went to Catholic school I was an atheist before I even graduated. The irony was not lost on me.

One of the more annoying effects of bipolar disorder is the grandiosity. I have feelings of greatness when manic but thankfully, I can't get any visits or direction from God. But I can easily see how people who believe in a god can feel like they're getting instruction from the Creator of the Universe when they're manic. Both mania and depression have very physical manifestations and you can't just 'calm down' any more than you can 'lighten up'. When you're flooded with a bunch of chemicals that you can't stop it's no stretch to think that you might be touched by God.

According to Christians, Jews and Muslims there was this guy named Moses who claimed to have regular conversations with God, and if you read even a little about him you'll find his body count is in the thousands.

Still, he is a revered figure among the three major religions. People were less evolved back then and it's easy to see how there was little to choose from in the way of religious leaders. It's the fact that they are still revered today that's so troubling.

Moses led a bunch of former slaves out of Egypt and promised to take them to their very own land of Israel. Along the way there was a lot of carnage, like the time he and his crew killed a bunch people who questioned his authority and when asked about it he said God made him do it.

He parked his people at the base of Mount Sanai with the strict instruction that nobody was allowed to go up the mountain without his permission. On his first trip up the mountain a couple years earlier, which was for forty days and forty nights, he met God in the form of a burning bush. Now, God came to him in a dream and summoned him again up the mountain for another meeting. This time he came down with a couple of stone tablets with a bunch of writing on them. What he saw when he came down threw him into such a rage he smashed the tablets. His people were partying like it was 1999 BC, dancing around a golden calf as if it were Spring Break. He dispatched his sons to kill a bunch of people as a warning to everyone, about three thousand people, including kids. It's right there in the bible like it was a good thing. He threw a hissy and marched straight back up the mountain for another forty days. When he came down this third time, everybody was properly reverent and listened obediently (and scared shitless) as he read them his new-

Ten Commandments

1. **I am the Lord your God,** who brought you out of the land of Egypt, out of the house of bondage.
2. **You shall have no other gods before me.** You shall not make for yourself a carved image, or any likeness of anything that is in heaven above, or that is in earth beneath, or that is in the water under the earth; you shall not bow down to them nor serve them. For I, the Lord your God, am a jealous and insecure God, visiting the iniquity of the fathers on the children to the third and fourth generations of those who don't like me, and showing mercy unto thousands of them that love me and keep my commandments.
3. **You shall not take the name of the Lord your God in vain.** For the Lord will not hold him guiltless that taketh his name in vain.
4. **Remember the Sabbath, to keep it Holy.** Six days you shall labor and do all your work, the seventh day is the Sabbath of the Lord your God. In it you shall do no work; you, nor your son, nor your daughter, nor your male servant, nor your female servant, nor your cattle, nor your stranger who is within your gates.
5. **Honor your father and mother,** that your days may be long upon the land which the Lord your God is giving you.
6. **You shall not kill.**
7. **You shall not commit adultery.**
8. **You shall not steal.**
9. **You shall not bear false witness against your neighbor.**

10. **You shall not covet your neighbor's house;** you shall not covet your neighbor's wife, nor his ass, nor his wife's ass, nor his male servant, nor his female servant, nor his ox, nor his monkey, nor anything else.

Ask anybody to list the Ten Commandments and chances are they will start off with 'Thou shalt not kill', as if that might be the most important sin a person should avoid. But of course, it's number 6.

The first three are all about what a pathetic jerk God is. He's supposed to be the Creator of the Universe but he sounds more like a vindictive eighth-grader-

'For I, the Lord your God, am a jealous and insecure god, visiting the iniquity of the fathers on the children to the third and fourth generations of those who don't like me...'

Number 4, about not working on Sundays, has never been taken seriously by all but the craziest of religious zealots even though it's supposed to be the goddamn WORD OF GOD.

And number 5 had to be aimed at his kids. Imagine your crazy eighty-year old dad going up a mountain to talk to a burning bush, and then slaughtering thousands of people in a fit of rage because they were having a party. You'd probably say something, like, 'Hey, Dad, maybe you should take it easy, huh? You can't be killing everybody in sight and claiming to talk to God. It makes you look crazy, you big nut...' So Moses, as a way to shut up his kids, made number 5, Honor your father and mother.

Number 6, Do not kill. Number SIX.

These are the same 10 Commandments that some people still fight to put up in schools and courtrooms and they were written by a crazy man, most likely an untreated manic depressive.

But he was hardly alone. The bible is full of figures who psychologists would quickly diagnose as mentally ill. Abraham damn near kills his son on a dare from God and Noah builds an ark and fills it full of wild animals. Jesus, the main character, is the definition of bipolar. His bouncing back and forth between fits of rage and crushing sadness is textbook manic depression. He thought he was the Son of God and as he was dying upon the cross, he yelled at God for forsaking him. I feel bad for Jesus. If he were born today he'd likely be on lithium and holding down a decent job as a productive member of society. Instead, he was crucified at 33 and now he's treated like a dead rock star by billions of people.

The most bipolar character ever created, of course, is God. The whole Old Testament is full of stories of a Creator who is an emotional wreck. Wiping out entire cities and mercilessly testing people like Job just to impress Satan. God is completely irrational and arbitrary to even his most loyal followers but he's worshipped by all the major religions and can do no wrong. So why not a new religion? Why the hell not Scottish Buddhism?

Never having started a new religion before, I was unsure exactly how to go about it. People in bars are generally pretty receptive to Scottish Buddhism, but I was serious and if I was going to upstage Christianity, I needed more than the few drunks I recruited at the George and Dragon.

I was discussing the latest new insidious religious argument masquerading as science, 'intelligent design' with one of my converts at the bar. I had read that there was a debate coming up at Town Hall between some dude from the Discovery Institute, the douchebags behind intelligent design, and a professor from the University of Washington. We guessed it would probably be an interesting exchange so we decided to make a presence. But how?

"We could streak it," he suggested.

There are times in life when you have the opportunity to do something that you will proudly look back on for the rest of your days. This would be major. And what better way to launch Scottish Buddhism than by disrupting a debate about religion with the undeniable proof that Scottish Buddhists were NOT intelligently designed? No matter how it went down, this was quite possibly going to be the greatest thing I would ever do.

One of my housemates, Serena (not her real name), was one of the naked bicyclists in the Fremont Solstice parade and she said she could produce a half dozen willing participants, easy. That was good because even though I now had a Scottish Buddhist Recruitment Center downtown, nobody was taking me seriously. And when someone actually did express interest in the Cause, when I mentioned that they were going to have to run naked through a public forum they would treat me like I was crazy and leave. The only woman who actually signed up quickly crossed my name off my enrollment list when I told her.

The debate was a week away when Serena's mother showed up from Texas. I liked her immediately and when I asked what brought her to Seattle, she looked at me like I must have been joking. "Serena's having a manic episode. You haven't noticed?"

As a matter of fact, I hadn't. Serena was also bipolar and she was certainly very animated lately, but I was always happy to see her like that. We were good friends and I hated it when she was depressed and cloistered in her room, alone.

I was feeling pretty lively myself and we spent many nights up late, plotting. She started a design firm in the basement and not only was I humoring myself with the whole Scottish Buddhism thing, I was now also running the Production Dept for my friend Steven's Utilikilt business. She brought home a dead rabbit she found in a park and put it in the freezer, and I hung a dead Jesus head from my bedroom ceiling.

So it didn't seem like anything was out of the norm, and I was a little surprised that Fay would come all the way up here just because our other housemates and her friends told Fay that Serena was being a little weird. Personally, I thought that being a teacher in Texas and flying up to Seattle in the middle of summer school just because your daughter said she might be divine was a little odd, but there it was.

And since timing is everything, it would only make sense that my plan to officially launch Scottish Buddhism by streaking through an auditorium with a bunch of other naked people would fail to happen because my friend and fellow housemate would have a mental breakdown a week too soon.

Serena got committed and I went to the debate alone. I made a sign and stood out front like a dork while almost everybody ignored me. Inside, I was able to ask a few pointed questions that made the intelligent design guy a little uncomfortable, but instead of any feelings of pride or amusement, I just felt sad that we, as a people, were still even talking about religion as if were any more debatable than the existence of Santa Claus.

Outside, I stood with my sign and hung out with some guy in a gorilla costume who was jumping up and down with a crucifix. In between various interactions with people filing out of auditorium, I asked the gorilla where he stood on the whole intelligent design thing, because, well... I was a little confused by his get-up.

"I don't know," he told me. "I just thought it would be fun to get stoned and wear my gorilla suit."

The Eleven Demandments of Scottish Buddhism

1. Live fully. It's better to regret the things you've done than the things you haven't. And it's a lot more fun.

2. Do not lie. Lies are too difficult to keep track of. Besides, the truth hurts, use it.

3. Quit thinking there's an afterlife. You get one chance to live, so suck it up and stop hoping there's a happy ending, there's not. Deal with it.

4. Admit that there is no god. Even if there WERE some 'supreme being' that created the universe and all the life forms on this planet, it certainly wouldn't give a shit about your pathetic little existence.

5. Accept that you were not meant to do anything.
There is no fate, only opportunity.
You were not put on this earth,
you just happen to be here.

6. Give away your crap. Materialism is shameful.
Plus, it's too expensive and it cuts
into the beer budget.

7. Take care of yourself. Your body is a temple, so always keep the basement clean because you never know when someone might want to go down there.

8. Don't be a dick. Try to be tolerant. How other people live their life is none of your freaking business. People should be allowed to live however they choose.
Except the Campbells.
Fuck them assholes.

9. Study dogs. They understand happiness.
Watch them and learn from them.

10. Do not celebrate holidays. Every day is special and should be spent well. Do not recognize the date of your birth. It is irrelevant.
In Scottish Buddhism you are ageless.

11. Wear comfortable shoes and clean socks.
You can't be productive if your feet hurt and you certainly won't get laid if they stink.

Carnitas

These are so good I once made nothing but carnitas for over a year and a half.

Needed-
Butter
Onion
Garlic
Pork loin
Orange
Refried beans
Extra sharp cheddar cheese
Jalapenos, pickled
Flour tortillas
Sour cream
Hot sauce
Cinnamon
Cilantro, guacamole, salsa or whatever else you might put in your carnitas

Prepare the Pot (see page 18)

When the pot is ready, add the pork. Sprinkle in some cinnamon, poke the hell out of the orange and add to the pot. Cook for a couple hours on **High** and then at least another 4 hours on **Low**.

Empty a can of refried beans into a pan and cover it with cheese. Cook in the oven until the cheese starts to get crispy. Warm the tortillas, even if it's just by putting them in foil on top of the crock pot. Tortillas are better warm.

Suggested beverage- Pike Place Pale Ale.

Stinkfoot

I took a job working for Steven as the Production Manager at his company, Utilikilts, but my feet were a problem. I hate buying clothes and for the most part, almost everything I have ever was either given to me or bought second hand. I'd been wearing a pair of used boots Steven had picked up at Value Village for me for the past year to replace a pair of boots that I'd worn for way too long.

But now the boots were not only coming apart, they stunk like a dead rodent and caused my feet to burn with pain. And they cost me a night of sex with Bridget and another night with some girl named Mary. It was time to do something.

I dropped my boots in the dumpster and walked around my office and the factory in my socks. Valerie, as usual, gave me a full ration of shit about it. Larry, our General Manager and Utilikilt's token Christian, pulled me aside and, ever the patient administrator, asked me what the hell I was doing.

I told Larry that my shoes were killing me and I couldn't wear them anymore. When he asked why I didn't get some new ones, I explained that I never had any time 'cause I was at work twelve hours a day and I had to take the bus because I gave my car away to one of the sewers. Besides, I'm not paying the kind of money they want for footwear nowadays.

What I meant was that as the Rama Lama of Scottish Buddhism, one of my perks was that other people were supposed to clothe and feed me. I was making forty thousand dollars a year as the Production Manager but that was beside the point. I genuinely believed that if I was going to go to the trouble of starting the next major world religion other people should have to chip in.

Larry gave Valerie forty bucks and asked her to take me to get some shoes.

She asked me where I wanted to go and I told her Fred Meyer's in Ballard. She made an unpleasant noise at the prospect of even driving into that part of town. She lived in Belltown and from her perspective, might just as well have been asked to drive into Watts.

But there was NO WAY she was gonna take me ANYWHERE if I wasn't wearing shoes.

"They can't kick me out for not wearing shoes if I'm there to buy shoes. That's ridiculous."

She told me in no uncertain terms that I had to dig my boots out of the garbage before she'd take me anywhere. She was always happy to get out from behind her desk, and I know she genuinely cared about the state of my feet, but for some reason, she was not about to walk into a department store with a man in a kilt and no shoes. Valerie is an only child and, I'm sure she would admit, thinks of me as the idiot brother she never had. So with a mild sense of duty (and to a certain extent, amusement) she took me to get shoes.

We walked through the shoe department and I grabbed the first pair of size 10½ comfortable looking shoes at $34.99 I saw. I put them on and they were perfect.

"Done," I said, heading for the check out. "Let's go."

Valerie, being a woman, was not impressed with how fast and easy shopping could be. "Put them back in the box. You're not wearing them up to the register. C'mon, I'm buying you some foot spray."

I put the shoes back in the box and followed her to the section where they keep all the foot care products. She was in the middle of trying to figure out if I needed a spray, a powder, or something more intensive like a two-week ointment treatment, when she looked down and noticed my stocking feet. She was livid. Worse than I had ever seen.

"Where are your shoes?!?!", she demanded. I offered up the new box of Sketchers but I couldn't say anything 'cause I was afraid I might laugh. "I swear to god if you don't go get your shoes right now I will leave you here. I am NOT kidding!" She grabbed the shoebox out of my hands and pointed towards the shoe department.

People were starting to look at us and I thought she might calm down a little bit. Instead, she grabbed my arm and pinched. Hard. I thought the growing number of interested fellow shoppers might keep her in check but she was surprisingly unconcerned with all the people looking at us. She raised some Desinex in a threatening manner and I plodded back to my old shoes, which were right on the floor where I left them.

The boots were so far gone I had stopped lacing them weeks ago. I hated that I had to put them on just to get out of the store so I dragged my feet and tried to look as pathetic as possible when I found her at the registers. I stopped five feet in front of her and asked for the shoes.

"Just let me have my shoes. I'll put the old ones in the box. Nobody will care, I promise. I looked at a sales clerk and was about to ask if it was okay if I swap out my shoes when Valerie realized she no longer needed me and set the shoes and foot ointment on the counter and thrust a bunch of bills at the cashier.

"Ignore him," she said. "He'll probably just follow me out."

the
12 STEP PROGRAM
for
CHRISTIANS

(and Muslims, Jews, Buddhists,
Hindus, Agnostics, etc, etc...)

So you want to be
a Scottish Buddhist...

You have grown disenchanted with your religion.

Of course you have. It was inevitable. You are an intelligent and inquisitive person, and as you have grown older you have naturally begun to question your faith. Not to do so would be irresponsible.

Whether you grew up a Christian, a Jew, a Muslim or that weird one that worships cows, the beliefs of your parents and grandparents have ultimately become suspect.

Or perhaps you have already grown disillusioned with your former religion and turned to 'traditional' Buddhism, thinking it offered Wisdom and Enlightenment just because it seems more introspective and serene. And although 'traditional' Buddhism got it the closest, it missed the mark with its multiple gods, its reincarnation, and the hopelessly misguided concept of 'karma', which implies a sense of order to the universe.

Wrong!

The time has come to throw away your rosary beads, your menorah, your Koran, and/or your colorful but pointless Tibetan prayer flags.

The Scottish Buddhist Twelve Step Program for Recovering Christians

1. Admit that you are powerless over the crushing reality of your limited existence. But you're not alone, for whatever that's worth.

2. Renounce your religion. Just because you were raised by Christians doesn't make it right. What if your parents believed in Santa Claus, would you believe that, too? Of course not.

3. Reach for a little perspective. No matter how bad your life might feel sometimes, it's nothing compared to what billions of people have dealt with for thousands of years. You're lucky to have the problems you have.

4. Take stock of your life. No one else is responsible for it and no one but you will suffer the consequences for wasting it.

5. Adopt a pet. Being responsible for the life of a dependent animal makes you a better person.

6. Accept that you will ALWAYS have to improve your character. Until you die, of course, then you won't have to do anything.

7. Take better care of yourself. Especially if you have kids. Or siblings or parents or friends. It's not all about you, you know.

8. Be nice. Make a conscious and deliberate effort to be a kind person.

9. Apologize to the people you've wronged, and MEAN IT.

10. Make a sacrifice. Nothing worthwhile is free, especially Scottish Buddhism.

11. Face it, everything's better with bagpipes. And the drone of the bagpipe is the perfect Ohm for meditating, if you're into that crap.

12. Go get shitfaced drunk. Congratulations-

You are now a Scottish Buddhist!

Scottish Eggs

Scottish eggs are a little tricky to make but once you master them you will be revered by your friends.

A Scottish egg is an egg that has been hard-boiled, encased in ground sausage, and then deep-fried. It is delicious and they're even better when they are coated in batter and deep-fried again and served with maple syrup.

Needed-
Eggs
Ground sausage
Cooking oil
Flour
Breadcrumbs

Hard boil several eggs and peel. Try soft boiling some eggs as well because even though it's difficult to peel them, the only thing better than a Scottish egg is a Scottish egg with a runny yolk.

Mix a pound and a half of ground sausage with one egg and a dash of flour. Put some flour on your hands and pack the sausage around the peeled eggs and roll them in breadcrumbs. Heat enough oil in a large pan to fit several eggs, at least 300 degrees if you have a thermometer. It's best if they are fully submerged but you can just keep turning them over if you don't have a big enough pan.

Cook for about five minutes or until brown.

Suggested beverage- Pike Place Pale Ale.

Nobody Respects the Scottish Inquisition

My friend Ray emailed me one day to tell me that he was now the curator for a new art space, and asked if I could think of an installation for it. I thought about it for a minute and replied-

"How about a Scottish Inquisition?"

"Perfect!"

He showed me the space the next day. It was a street level space in the corner of another newly built condominium complex in the soulless Seattle neighborhood called Belltown. The dimensions were odd and not exactly suited to just any art installation. It was about forty feet wide, five feet deep, and the height varied from about ten to twenty feet.

But it would be ideal for what I would need. I looked around and imagined a venue for overthrowing Christianity, removing then-president Bush from power, displaying my bagpipes and, hopefully meeting some chicks.

"So," Ray said. "They're having a little get-together at Hugo House's Writer's Cottages just a couple blocks from here. Let's go get a drink."

"Sure!" As we walked, we discussed the details.

It would be a recruitment center, storage depot, and launching site for the Scottish Buddhist Uprising.

The first section (there were three) would be a showcase for my bagpipes. The second would be interactive- I could set up an information booth and hand out fliers. The third would be reserved for stockpiling kilts, comfortable shoes, beer, Serenity maces, and whatever else would be needed.

"Cool," Ray said as we arrived at the cottages and he poured me a glass of wine. They were having their quarterly meeting and were about to hear from me. "Tell it to them."

Somebody was talking about the future direction of the Hugo House and how they hoped to be more involved in the arts. "Which brings us to Ray," the person said, noticing Ray as we sat down.

He took a drink and stood up. He said something or other about performance art and involvement and whatnot, but it was obvious that he was about to hand the floor over to me, so I downed my wine.

"...which brings us to Jay."

I stood up and looked around. Gray hair, black blouses, manicured beards, turquoise...

I had the sudden feeling that most of the people there had actually known about this night beforehand and would be expecting something. It was also the night that the founder and director of the organization was passing the torch to her successor, which unfortunately meant that it was a full house.

"Um," I began. "Everybody talks about religion, but nobody ever does anything about it."

Silence.

I stumbled through a presentation and was fully aware of Ray's inability to keep a straight face. But I pulled out everything I had about Scottish Buddhism and the impending Uprising (I left out the part about potentially toilet-papering the church around the corner), and they seemed to warm up a little.

A couple more people spoke about different things while I drank their wine and nibbled their cheeses. Afterwards, we all walked back to the art space and the board members, writers, artists, and supporters asked their questions and, somewhat grudgingly, mostly, gave their endorsements.

It was on.

Ray printed up a 3' x 6' version of the Eleven Demandments and some signage, and provided boxes that he labeled 'kilts', 'shoes', and 'pamphlets'.

I set up a table with a sign that said 'Ask me about Scottish Buddhism.'

We made picket signs that said things like-

Scottish Buddhists are NOT
Intelligently Designed

and

If it's not SCOTTISH Buddhism, it's CRAP!

This all came about at a very fucked up time in my life. Eight months earlier I had given up my boat business and gone to work for my friend Steven as we set up a factory for his kilt business. Running the factory was the most fun job I ever had but, for whatever reason, we couldn't work together without wanting to kill each other, so I quit. I've got a full story about my time at Utilikilts but every time I start to write it, it just comes out bitter and mean, which isn't very Scottish Buddhist.

This was also when my housemate Serena had her manic meltdown and had to be committed for a few weeks. This came at the unfortunate time of the renewal of our lease and the owners decided they would rather find a nice family to rent their house than to deal with the likes of us anymore.

So here I was- jobless, broke and homeless. And expected to form some stupid new religion that was supposed to overthrow Christianity. Perfect.

I had a little bit of time to reflect on things as I sat at my table, waiting for people to ask me about Scottish Buddhism. Most people just looked at me funny as they passed but some actually asked me what the hell I was doing. I usually just handed them a copy of the Eleven Demandments or the 12 Step Program or a beer and got back to reading my book or doing my crossword.

One day Serena's mother got ahold of me and asked if I would go with her to visit Serena in the mental hospital in West Seattle. I said I would, as long as it was okay with Serena. I called the hospital and they actually let me talk to her.

"Please come get me, Jay. This is no place for somebody who's on the edge..."

I told her I would come and bust her out of there. "Are you gonna beat people up?" she asked me. I promised her I wouldn't hurt anybody and told her to gather her things. Her mom and I would be there in a couple hours. We had to take the bus because a couple weeks earlier I had given away my car.

Serena and I had met about a year and a half earlier when I answered an ad on CraigsList. She was looking for new housemates because all the previous ones had moved out all at once, and I needed a new place because the former Zen center wasn't the same since Sunshine left to sell medicinal herbs in San Francisco.

Elena, Debbie and I moved in with Serena in the Wallingford neighborhood of Seattle. It was about a five minute drive from Ballard but I thought that living out in the 'burbs might be healthy for me. Perhaps if I had to commute home to Wallingford everyday, I might be more responsible.

I embraced my new communal household. I microwaved burritos while Serena cooked her tofu and vegan food. I made peanut butter and pineapple jelly sandwiches while Elena cooked her New Jersey Italian food (every meal had a hard boiled egg!). And I ate burritos and peanut butter and jelly sandwiches while Debbie made her kosher meals. They all seemed to enjoy company and even fed me things other than burritos and sandwiches.

One night I was lying in bed, listening to the radio, reading a book, and most certainly NOT out drinking and doing something stupid. Serena had been pretty reclusive, so I was happy when she knocked on my door and came and sat on my bed. She seemed a little disconnected, and she needed to talk to somebody. She told me she was manic depressive. Bipolar.

From then on we were tight. So when either of us had one of our little battles, the other one would be there, hopefully, to provide a potential dose of reality.

Now I was gonna spring her from the loony bin.

Fay and I took a bus and ended up walking a half a mile in the rain. It bothered me that she had to deal with the serious mental breakdown of her child. I had been prepared to bust Serena free but now I was more concerned for her mother. She was on the verge of tears and I tried to be stable. We were brought up to the third floor and it was beyond disturbing...

I remembered somebody once telling me about how easy it is to go crazy. All you have to do is just let go. You don't have to care about what other people think of you. You don't have to worry about anything in the future and you can forget about everything in the past. Just let go...

Fay and I got off the elevator and walked into a clusterfuck of blue pajamas and security aides with photo IDs. Serena was watching from down the hall and laughing to herself. She had warned anyone who would listen that the Rama Lama was coming to bust her out and if they were smart they would get the hell out of there.

I was completely drenched, wearing a Boat Fetish T-shirt and a work kilt. I'm a little stocky with gray hair and a red beard. As I walked up to Serena, I felt watched. We talked quietly but I was feeling increasingly paranoid. Her mother and a cadre of guards were obviously talking about us.

I was suddenly in a very bad place. I felt prone. I had gone there with the intention of getting her out, and now I was beginning to wonder if I'd be walking out myself. She was right, this certainly was no place for somebody on the edge. I was homeless, unemployed, trying to enlist an army of Scottish Buddhists and now... what? It was almost like I could feel insanity crawling up my leg.

Serena told me everything and more about what she was going through. She was the daughter of God (Fay was an imposter)... her reality was simply temporarily disjointed and there was no fucking WAY she was gonna take those pills... something about the government...something about testing me to see if I was a spy... And she asked to borrow a pen which she tried to hide in her sleeve but was immediately retrieved by an aide.

I suggested that maybe she should just try to play along and not say anything nutty and maybe they'd let her out. "You don't have to say every thought that comes through your head," I told her. "Jesus. If I told these guys even a little bit of the shit I've told you they'd give me my own room."

We hatched a quick plan and were good to go. I went and talked to Fay as Serena gathered her belongings in a pillowcase.

Soon her mother and I were getting back in the elevator and, on cue, Serena rushed the closing door. She threw her sack at my feet and tried kicking her way in as Security pulled her out and the doors closed. They easily dragged her away and I yelled for her to "Play their game, Serena! Just tell them what they want to hear so you can get out of here!"

Fay and I rode the elevator down and I was completely disoriented. Fay is about the sweetest person I have ever met and she just witnessed her daughter trying to barge her way out of a mental institution.

The ride back downtown was excruciating. I had no idea what to say, but fortunately, Fay probably wasn't expecting too much from me in the way of advice, anyway. She maintained her way through the twenty minute bus ride as we stumbled between small talk, a couple attempts at discussing her daughter's mental illness, and silence.

We parted by the Pike Place Market and I went back to my Uprising. I picked up a six-pack and sat alone, unbothered as I read my book.

About a week later, Serena called me from the hospital. She was completely lucid. "They got me back on my meds. I'm okay again. I'm getting out tomorrow," she told me. "I remember that you came here with my Mom but I don't really remember much about it..."

Double Deep-Fried Scottish Eggs

<u>Needed-</u>
Scottish eggs
1 cup flour
1 tablespoon baking powder
1 teaspoon salt
½ cup milk
½ cup water
Maple syrup

Mix the flour, baking powder and salt together in a bowl, and then add in the water and milk. Mix well and then roll a Scottish egg in it until it is fully covered. Drop it in the oil and cook until done, maybe three to four minutes.

Serve with maple syrup.

Bring these to a brunch and people will rave about you for the rest of their lives.

Suggested beverage- Pike Place Kilt Lifter Scottish Ale.

How (and Why) to Make a Bagpipe

After my buddy Dave died and my wife left me I made a serious effort to grow my business and sell Huggy Jesus dolls to the Christians. But the economy crashed after 9/11 and I did, too, as I fell into yet another deep depression. I closed my business and found a small shop in the Fenpro building in Ballard. I had hired a bagpiper for Dave's memorial and still, the wail of the chanter and drone of the pipes lingered. I decided to fill the world with bagpipes.

I started building crazy looking composite bagpipes and my mania kicked in hard. I made the Guinness pipes, the Orange Protest pipes, the Racing pipes, the first set of Percussion pipes (a two-man bagpipe that's also a drum kit) and a set made from driftwood.

It took me a few years to figure out how to make a fully functional Great Highland bagpipe out of brass tubing, fiberglass and carbon fiber. It also took me about that long to figure out there is no market for funky looking, non-traditional bagpipes. The problem is that most bagpipers hate them.

Because a bagpipe is such a difficult instrument to play, piping is more like an exact science than an art. Pipers are trained in the strict structure of a traditional pipe band where there is no room for variation of any kind. The majority of pipers want nothing to do with my funky looking bagpipes and they are the only ones who can play them and since I can't play them they're pretty much useless. I've made ten so far and only sold one. The rest I gave away, except for the Green Marble pipes (which I'll never sell) and the Pictish War pipes, which are two life-sized legs covered with tribal tattoos and blue dye. I don't know what to do with those.

The pipes I make are too complicated to make at home. My friend Denny made me some tools to make a few brass fittings that aren't available anywhere and all the soldering is kind of a pain in the ass.

So I came up with a way to make a fully functional Great Highland bagpipe out of PVC pipe and nylon tubing. It looks like it was ripped out of your bathroom but they sound as good as any bagpipe you will ever come across. For a tenth of the cost.

So here is a detailed description of how to build a bagpipe. To get started you will need the following-

<u>PARTS LIST</u>   <u>Cut lengths</u>
A- Nylon tube .250 ID x .375 OD

Bottoms- bass		12 3/8"
tenors	2@ 9 3/8"	18 3/4"
Blow pipe		<u>9"</u>
		40"

B- Nylon tube .375 ID x .500 OD

Bass middle		7 1/2"
Bottom & spacers	8@ 2"	<u>16"</u>
		23 1/2"

C- Nylon tube .500 ID x .562 OD

Bass middle spacers	2@ 2"	4"

D- Nylon tube .562 ID x .625 OD

Tops- bass		7"
tenors	2@ 4"	8"
Bass middle		7 1/2"
Bottoms- bass		13"
tenors	2@10"	<u>20"</u>
		55 1/2"

E- PVC pipe .800 ID (sold as 3/4 ID)

Tops- bass		12"
tenors	2@ 9"	18"
Bass middle		7"
Bottoms- bass		7"
tenors	2@ 4"	8"
Stocks - bass		7 1/2"
tenors	2@ 5 1/2"	11"
blowpipe, chanter	2@3 1/2"	<u>7"</u>
		77 1/2"

F- clear plastic hose .375 OD

<u>PLUS-</u>   <u>TOOLS-</u>
3/4" to 1" brass fittings (3)   Pipe cutter, calipers
3/8" metal washers (3)   Razor blade, round file
Electrical tape, plastic cement

The Great
Highland Bagpipe

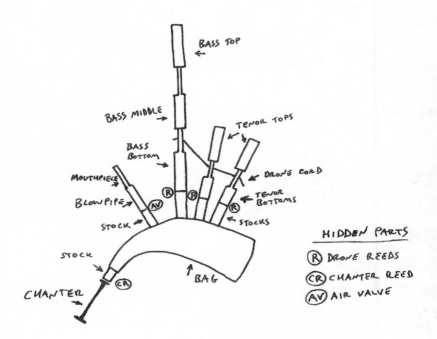

BASS TOP

BASS MIDDLE

TENOR TOPS

BASS BOTTOM

DRONE CORD

MOUTHPIECE

TENOR BOTTOMS

BLOWPIPE

STOCK

STOCKS

STOCK

BAG

CHANTER

HIDDEN PARTS

(R) DRONE REEDS

(CR) CHANTER REED

(AV) AIR VALVE

Corned Beef Hash

I decided to get a dog. Not just for the companionship and because there was a dog who needed a home, but because it would make me more responsible if I had to go home to walk my dog instead of staying out drinking. I found him through a rescue but had to wait a few weeks before I could take him in case his owners claimed him.

Meanwhile, I came up with a recipe we would both enjoy. On Sundays we would go for a walk and get the paper and some groceries. Back on the boat we would watch football and cook up a big pot of food to sustain us for the week.

Needed-
Butter
Onion
Garlic
3 pounds of corned beef
4 large potatoes
2 eggs
Catsup
Salt and pepper

Prepare the Pot (see page 18)

Cut up the corned beef into small manageable pieces. When the pot is ready, add the corned beef and cook on Low for two hours, mashing it around and letting it sizzle. Add in the potatoes and eggs. Throw in a little catsup and some salt and pepper, mash well and turn the pot to Low for another 6 hours.

Suggested beverages- Redhook ESB, water

Disneyland

After Utilikilts, I went back to working on boats and spent about six months living out of a car. I managed to buy a small boat to live on, got a crock pot, started writing, and got a rescue dog I named Kenny, after my father. And then my sister, Suzi, gave me some work writing trivia questions for Trivial Pursuit and Family Feud.

Suzi had been doing trivia part time for the Hasbro company for a few years and as she had gotten busy with her marketing gig, she was more than happy to give me the work. And I loved it. I spent a full year lazing about my boat writing trivia and beginning what would become the Scottish Buddhist Cookbook.

Hasbro first wanted 1,000 questions with four multiple-choice answers for their new online version of Trivial Pursuit. The topics were History, Music, Science, TV, things like that. It was easy and fun.

Once those were done, they gave us 10,000 original trivia questions and answers and asked for three new wrong answers, or 'misleads' for each question, paying us $2 per question. They gave us questions like, Who was Mother Theresa?, and I gave answers like a French chef, a TV clown, or a Russian prostitute. They asked, What US president, upon taking office, first learned about the existence of the atomic bomb? It was Harry S Truman, but I offered Franklin Roosevelt, Dwight Eisenhower and George W Bush. You'd think I might have learned a lot but unfortunately I'm just as likely to remember a wrong answer as the correct one.

But then came a few thousand questions for Family Feud where they provided the question and the first four most obvious answers. I then had to come up with eight more probable answers to questions like- Name something you do with your teeth. Survey says- you can brush them and floss them and pick them and whiten them. Now, for two dollars, name another eight things you can do to your teeth. Now imagine answering a hundred of those questions every day for two months without popping your eyes out with your thumbs.

Suzi was going through her divorce at the time and thought that what she really needed was a road trip with her big brother and a certain Scottish Buddhist terrier. I'm always up for a road trip and when I asked where she wanted to go she said she didn't care, just somewhere that involved driving through a desert.

I was reading Jon Krakauer's *Under the Banner of Heaven* at the time and when I started to mention that maybe we could go to Utah to check out the Mormons she said YES! before I could even finish the sentence. She flew out to Seattle and we spent a few days researching both the Latter Day Saints and their estranged Fundamentalist offspring.

We got a couple more books- *Escape* by Carolyn Jessup and *Lost Boy* by Brent Jeffs, and spent a couple days reading and researching online. I put something on Facebook that we'd like to find somebody to crash with for a couple nights while we were there. A friend vouched for me and a generous family offered to put us up. Brian and Karen grew up Mormons and welcomed us into their home like family.

We rented a car because my truck at the time got about four miles to the gallon, and we headed to Salt Lake City. On the road to Utah we discovered that authors Carolyn and Brent were both on Facebook and were more than willing to meet with us and discuss their books. We also stocked up on beer and vodka for obvious reasons and Suzi bought a video camera to get some footage and record some interviews because the more we looked into the Fundamentalist Mormons, the more fascinating it was.

When the Mormons decided to renounce polygamy, they said it was because God decided it was no longer necessary. Coincidently, it was at the same time the US government said it was mandatory for them to renounce polygamy if they wanted statehood for Utah, which they desperately did. This didn't mean that they fully stopped practicing polygamy, it just meant they had to tone it down and be more discreet about it. And while there are many Mormons who regard polygamy as an ugly stain on their religion and want nothing to do with it, there have always been many who firmly believe that plural marriage is essential to enter the Kingdom of Heaven.

During the Great Depression a group of disgruntled Mormons formed the Fundamental Church of Jesus Christ of Latter Day Saints, the FLDS, and moved to a remote piece of land on the border of Utah and Arizona that they called Short Creek where they could freely practice polygamy, or Celestial Marriage. They also set up something called the United Effort Plan, which was sold as both a way to pool their resources in tough times and to rid the flock of the selfishness of owning such earthly extravagances as land and a house.

Short Creek, or Hildale, Utah and Colorado City, Arizona as it appears on a map, has always been run by tyrannical assholes who called themselves prophets- Uncle Roy, Uncle Rulon, and Warren Jeffs. Now that Warren Jeffs is sitting in prison for arranging the marriage and subsequent rape of a fourteen year old girl, Short Creek is like a family fighting over a dead parent's estate. Many have relocated to Eldorado, Texas but those who stayed are either now under the rule of Merril Jessop or living as apostates, shunned by the church but refusing to leave their homes.

Carolyn's parents moved to the town of Hildale when she was a kid and Carolyn was forced to marry fifty-year-old Merril Jessop when she was eighteen. By thirty-five she had eight children and six 'sister wives'. She is also the first and only woman to escape the compound with all of her children. Six years later she was still fighting her ex-husband, now the current prophet and leader, for all kinds of custody and child support issues.

Suzi interviewed Carolyn, who also gave her a few other contacts. One was her friend Michelle, who had not only married into the FLDS, but still lives in Colorado City. Suzi called her and she was more than meet us and give us a tour of the compound.

We drove to St George, which is about five or six hours from Salt Lake, and about forty-five minutes outside of Colorado City. We got a room and decided to make a quick trip to the compound with for a drive-through before meeting Michelle the next morning. If you're going to start a community that is far from meddlesome gaze of the law, you can't do much better than Short Creek. It's nestled under a bluff out in the middle of the desert, just north of the Grand Canyon.

There are no welcome signs as you take the left turn off of Route 59 into Short Creek, only a sign to tell you that you are no on the border of Utah and Arizona. It was getting near dusk as we rolled past the dairy and into town. I felt a little nervous because of everything we'd read and been told about the place but it was also like entering a creepy theme park. I would have gladly paid $60 for a weekend pass if anybody would have just asked for it.

The roads are mostly dirt and the houses all seem to be works-in-progress. There was a park with nobody in it, but occasionally a woman or two with a few children in their front yards. I had to drive slow so Suzi could do her filming, but I was also thinking it would be nice to get back to St George, order a pizza, have some beers, and come back in the morning.

Across the street, in a parking lot of some sort, I saw a pickup truck pull into a parking spot. In the back were a couple women and a dozen kids. The women and girls wore the standard prairie dresses and the boys all had long sleeve shirts and long pants, even though it was about a hundred degrees. I thought Suzi should get some footage of this family and started to tell her so when she screamed "LOOK OUT!" and I slammed on the brakes before very nearly running over a little boy who was darting across the street to meet the family getting out of the bed of the truck.

After a couple deep breaths, I pulled a uey and carefully made it back out of the compound and onto the highway. There was no need to speak about what might have happened had I killed a little FLDS boy while sight-seeing in their compound, so we said nothing on the drive back to St George. Back at the hotel I drank every beer I had and half of Suzi's vodka before I was able to get to sleep.

There are actually three separate sects of fundamentalist Mormons on the border of Utah and Arizona. The first was the FLDS and their United Effort Plan. But the leadership of the fundamentalists has always been more political than religious, so two other groups left and built their own communities on the other side of the highway. There are the Tankers, or at least that's what the remaining residents of Short Creek call them because they have a water tank, and the Centennials. The Centennials left the FLDS in Short Creek decades ago and set up their compound just a couple miles down the road in a place they called Centennial Park. This group, who unapologetically practice polygamy, runs the Merry Wives Café, which is right across the street from the entrance to Short Creek. This is where we met Michelle, who showed up with her husband and a few of her kids.

Michelle grew up a Mormon, but the mainstream kind from Salt Lake City, not the magic underwear wearing kind from Short Creek. Her father used to tease her and her sisters growing up that if they weren't good he was going to drop them off at the Plygs, as they're sometimes called, and nobody would ever hear from them again. Instead, Michelle met Danielle, fell in love, and married into the FLDS.

Daniel grew up in Short Creek in a typical polygamist family. In his twenties he began building a house large enough for a full family. When he questioned something the leader Warren Jeffs said, Jeffs called him "The Worst Apostate That Ever Infected God's Earth. Worse Than Satan" and sent over some thugs from the police department to remove him from his own house. Jeffs then moved Daniel's brother into the house and Daniel left the compound for a few years. He only moved back to reclaim his house after Jeffs was arrested and thrown in prison.

There was no separation between the church and any other aspect of life in Short Creek, and when Jeffs was caught it not only threw the flock into complete disarray, it also made many of the residents deeply question what they believed. Some members saw it as God's Will and relocated to a new compound in Eldorado, Texas with Jeff's successor and Carolyn's former husband, Merrill.

Others remained loyal to Jeffs and felt like the world was ending, again, and holed up in their houses with the shades drawn for the next six months. During this time Short Creek looked like a ghost town. Parents only went outside for food and essentials and the children were subjected to Jeff's recorded sermons, over and over again as they awaited the Apocolypse. Michelle and Daniel and a couple dozen other families decided to stay and fight for the houses they built.

When Suzi first talked to her on the phone, Michelle was outgoing and funny, and when we met her outside the café I was a little disappointed that she wasn't wearing a prairie dress. But Michelle and Daniel never fit the profile of a typical FLDS couple. They've got five kids, but the whole polygamy thing was never an option. Michelle laughed at the idea of sharing her husband with a few other women and Daniel simply shuddered at it.

We followed them into the compound and they took us first to one of the two small parks in Short Creek. There was nobody there at first, and I held the camera while Suzi interviewed them. A teenager on an old bike rode past us a few times and then took off. With Suzi in her halter top and me in my kilt, it must have been cause for some alarm 'cause not ten minutes later a big black pickup truck with tinted windows slowly rolled by and parked down the street.

"That's just Hank, he's with the God Squad. He doesn't follow us around very much anymore, but he'll be watching you, that's for sure," Michelle told us. With Warren Jeffs in prison, the God Squad didn't have to anybody to report to but old habits die hard and now they're running mostly on paranoia. After hanging out with them for a couple hours and a tour of the compound with the black pickup following us around the whole time, we went to dinner at Uncle Marvin's.

Uncle Marvin had four wives and thirty-five children. His two main wives are Charlotte and Laura, who were both there, along with a couple dozen children and grandchildren. They were surprisingly open about their polygamist lives and the only thing they were pretty guarded about was their current beliefs. I was interested in what it was like in that environment, but what I really wanted to know was- What do you believe in now?

We sat around the table for probably three hours and I never got an answer. In the kitchen, covering one whole wall, were dozens of front pages and magazine covers dealing with Warren Jeffs' arrest. They were happy to talk about how Jeffs ruined their community and how they missed the way things were, but there didn't seem to be any consensus about where to go from here. It's been a couple years since Jeffs was convicted and, sitting among Marvin and Laura and Charlotte and several of their grown children, it was obvious that, apart from their oldest son David, who was now an atheist, nobody could really explain what they believed or no longer believed. They just wished things were the way they used to be, back when Uncle Roy was running things.

Warren Jeffs' father and predecessor, the Prophet Uncle Rulon, spoke many times about the End of the World, but each time the much anticipated Lifting Up, as they called it, came and went and each time the failure of the Rapture to take place was blamed on the congregation. Daniel remembers being yelled at by Uncle Rulon for not deserving the Apocolypse. They weren't righteous enough, yet.

The End was first supposed to happen in July of 1999, but that didn't happen so the date was pushed back to the obvious date of Y2K. This time they were serious and everybody in Short Creek began to make preparations. They prayed more and they were determined that this was really gonna be It. The Prophet told them that some of their children would not be Lifted 'cause they were brats and their parents obviously couldn't control them. The thought of leaving their children behind was too much for many of the mothers and a doctor in nearby St George stepped in with his prescription pad to help.

Michelle told us that every time you drove by the doctor's office you were likely to see an FLDSer sitting in his truck, waiting for his wives to come out with their mother's little helpers.

Since the End of the World was neigh, many families decided to live it up a little, much to the delight of the Ford truck dealer and the Best buy in St George and the ATV store in Hurricane. Credit cards were maxed out but it didn't matter. This last summer before the End of the World was gonna be the greatest!

And once again when the Apocolypse didn't happen, it was because they weren't worthy. On top of that, now they have truck payments they can't afford. Fortunately for Mormons, life on this planet is just one long difficult test but once it's over, it'll all be worth it. Getting your truck repossessed isn't that bad when you know that in your next life you'll get to be God and You can make Your own damn pickup truck that will be way better than an F-250 anyway.

But a serious problem for the FLDS is one of basic math. If you're a middle-aged man and require even the minimum three young wives, the last thing you need is a bunch of teenage boys around. So you systematically weed out as many young men as you can. When a boy turns thirteen and fourteen, he's got to start watching himself because every mistake he makes is one step closer to being kicked out of the compound. One of the biggest sins a boy can commit while growing up is to ever question authority and any evidence of that is all the Prophet needs to put your troublesome ass on a bus to St George. And try to imagine growing up your whole life being told that the Outside World is full of Evil and you'd get eaten alive out there and then all of a sudden you're cast out into it and your own parents don't do anything to stop it.

In the Book of Mormon, blacks are the descendants of Cain and native Americans are descendants of Laman, some dude who killed all the good Israelites who had sailed over to the Americas back around 600 BC, so they're no good either. And every other non-Mormon is a godless crook who will rape and murder you without a second thought. Just think about that when you've been banished and you're living under a bridge in Las Vegas, young man.

Suzi and I had a great time. All except for that one time in the car as we left St George for our first full day in the compound. She'd picked up a Utilikilt while in Seattle and as we were getting ready to leave the hotel room, she was actually wearing it! I knew she didn't know what she was doing. But when you're a dude in a kilt, you're just a dude in a kilt. When you're a dude in a kilt and there's a girl right next to you wearing the same thing, then you're a 'dude' walking into an ultra-conservative Fundamentalist Mormon compound in a skirt.

How to Make a Bass Middle

This is the hardest part to make when I make a set of composite Great Highland pipes so I always make this part first to get it out of the way. It can take days to make this part with brass tubing and then shaping it to look like something. But you make this part out five pieces of PVC and some electrical tape in about an hour.

Needed-
One B nylon tube @ 7 1/2"
One D nylon tube @ 7 1/2"
Two C nylon 2" spacers
One E PVC pipe @ 7"
Hot glue gun

Slide a C spacer on one end of the B tube and slide the D tube over it from the other end. Jam the second spacer in between the other ends of the tubes.

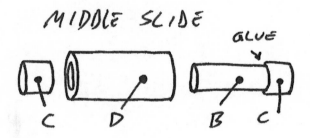

Measure the interior of the E pipe and wrap two bands of electrical tape on one end of the slide, one on the end 2 1/2" up. Now slide the E pipe on until it's snug and covers the tape, leaving 5" of the slide exposed. Add a nice bead of glue at the base of the slide and top of the PVC pipe.

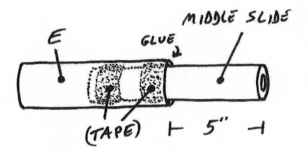

Pho

Pho is very easy to make, healthy (probably), women love it, and your dog gets a beef bone. Crock pot pho is the essence of Scottish Buddhism.

Needed-
Butter
Onion
Garlic
2 pounds beef bone and/or oxtail
Water
Spices
Green onion
Lime
Thin sliced roast beef
Rice noodles
Hoisin sauce
Chili paste
Salt
A bunch of reusable plastic containers
Pint glass
Chopsticks

Prepare the Pot (see page 18)

Put the beef bone and/or oxtail in the pot and fill almost to the top with water. Cook on **High** for at least 6 hours or preferably, on **Low** overnight.

Strain out all the bones and meat. Set aside a couple choice bones for your canine buddy, but make sure to let them cool for a while. Add some water to get the level back up to just under the brim, and any spices you might like. Cook on **High** for a little while longer. Strain out the broth into a bunch of reusable plastic containers and store in the fridge.

To prepare your pho-
Strain some broth into a pan and bring to a boil. Add in some rice noodle, some hoisin sauce, and a little chili paste. Bring it back to a boil, add a little salt, turn off the heat and let stand while you chop up some green onions and a wedge of lime. Squeeze the lime on slices of roast beef. Add the green onion and beef and pour into pint glasses. [A regular bowl is okay, but a pint glass keeps the pho hot longer.]

Suggested beverages- IPA.

How to Make a Drone Bottom

Needed-
One A nylon tube @ 12 3/8"
Two A nylon tubes @ 9 3/8"
Six B nylon spacers @ 2"
One D nylon tube @13"
Two D nylon tubes @ 10"
One E PVC pipe @ 7"
Two E PVC pipes @ 4"

Slide a B spacer on each end of the A tubes. Adjust so the spacers are flush with one side of the A tube and overhang by about 5/8" on the other. Give a bead of glue to the inboard edge of the spacers and let dry.

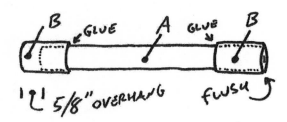

It'll take a little practice to get the Tape Wrapping down, but it's not that hard. Make sure the inside corners of the D tube are smooth and measure the inside diameter with the calipers. The whole point of putting the tape on is to both fill the space between the spacers and the D tube, and to make it a snug fit so things don't move around. Wrap the tape until it's the same diameter as the inside of the D tube and then force them together. It may take a few attempts but you'll figure it out. Now you have the slides-

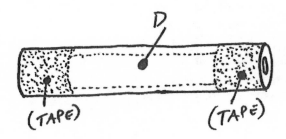

Now you're gonna put the E PVC pipes on. The E pipes sit up about 1 1/4" from the bottom end of the slides. This is so bottoms sit about 1 1/4" into the stocks when the bagpipe is assembled. Smooth the inside edges of the E pipe with a file and wrap the slide with tape. Make sure the side with the reed seat is the side that sits out 1 1/4".

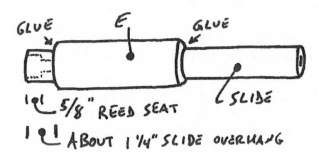

When all of the bottoms are put together give them beads of glue between the PVC and the slides.

How to Meditate

When I was in my twenties I could meditate easily and for long periods of time. It was the only useful thing I got out of traditional Buddhism, as all the rest of it is hopelessly locked in to karma and the idea that life never ends, which is ridiculous. There is no karma and when you die you're dead. The sooner you accept this the sooner you can get on with your life.

But as I got older it got harder and harder to turn my brain off long enough to clear my thoughts so I stopped trying to meditate altogether.

Then, when I constructed the very first set of playable bagpipes that I made, I got the drones going and kept them up for as long as I could, maybe a half hour.

And that's when I realized that the drone of the bagpipe provides the perfect ohm for meditating. All you have to do is close your eyes and keep a steady flow of air through the drones and that's all you need to get closer to the Truth than any monk in a red robe sitting in a cave has ever gotten. Ever. Never trust anybody who claims to have found Enlightenment after not eating for two months. That's crazy. How that whole religion got traction is the real Mystery of the Universe.

Scottish Buddhist Meditation may sound silly at first, but it makes more sense than trying to meditate WITHOUT a bagpipe. I'd bet anything that most people who pay to sit on a yoga mat and 'meditate' aren't meditating at all. They're thinking about Game of Thrones or trying to figure out what's for dinner. There's no faking it with bagpipes. Some people may be able to find serenity peacefully, but I think most of us need it blasted into us.

Tall Papa Bear's Shortbread for Scottish Buddhists

This recipe comes from my sister's friend named Skye that he stole from his dad whose name I don't know.

Needed-
8 oz whipped sweet butter
8 oz sugar (coarse can be blended with normal sugar)
27 oz unbleached baking flour
4 oz rice flour
Scale
Large stainless steel bowl
Wooden spoon
Pastry knife
Another bowl
Sifter
Fork
2 pie tins
Smooth block of wood
Pick
Ruler
Gas oven

Mix the whipped butter and sugar in the large stainless bowl using the wooden spoon and the pastry knife. Do not melt the butter, simply break it up into small bits.

Put the flour in the other bowl. Sift in the rice flour. Mix it really well. Use a fork and spin the bowl around to really mix it well. Seriously, mix it well.

Pour the mixed flours over the butter and sugar. Go wash your hands again. Mix by hand. This should be done in a cool environment because you don't want the butter to melt and become too oily. This is important.

From this batter create two equally sized large balls. Place each ball on a pie tin. Do NOT grease the tin.

Now comes the tough part-

The object here is to press the ball out from the center, rotating the ball out to 6". Press down with your palm as you rotate the pan. Use your thumb to work the batter out from the center. You must keep the rounding from breaking apart at the ends, so you have to pinch and smooth the ends. Carefully pound with the smooth wooden block until the batter is exactly 1/2" thick.

Using the pick, poke holes throughout the shortbreads. Triangular sections can be punched to make it easier to break apart after it's baked.

Sugar can be sprinkled on top of rounds before baking.

Set oven to 325 degrees.

Place rounds in the oven and bake for 50-55 minutes. You will have to be very mindful that you do not overbake them. Pay close attention at this point. If you don't pull them out at exactly the right time you might as well just throw them away.

Cool at Scottish room temperature (48 degrees).

Suggested beverage- Hot buttered cider.

How to Make a Drone Top

<u>Needed-</u>
One D nylon tube @ 7"
Two D nylon tubes @ 4"
One E PVC pipe @ 12"
Two E PVC pipes @ 9"
Three 3/4" to 1/2" brass reduction fittings
Three 3/8" metal washers

Put the brass reduction fittings on one end of each of the three D tubes and secure them with glue and a couple wraps of tape. Now add enough tape to the D tube on both ends so that it fits snugly inside the E pipe. The large D goes inside the large E, and the two smaller Ds go inside the two smaller Es, but you probably got that.

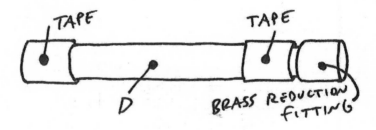

Glue the brass to the PVC. Now make yourself a quick little Cap Aligner to ensure that you put the metal cap on so that it is centered with the inner D tube. Do this with some tubing and tape. Slide the washer onto the brass and let it sit until the glue has set.

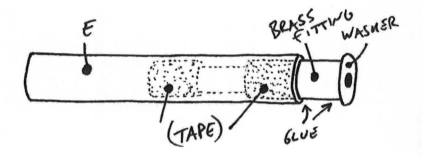

Hot Buttered Cider

<u>Needed-</u>
Apple cider
Rum
Butter
Cinnamon sticks

Bring a large amount of cider to a boil. Add rum, butter and cinnamon.

Alexander the Great, Undiagnosed Bipolar

To be a Duck Captain you need to get both a commercial drivers license and a special captains license from the US Coast Guard. Somewhere in the process I was asked if I was on any medication for any mental condition, like lithium for treating bipolar disorder.

I didn't want to lie, so I went off my meds.

I'd gone off medications several times before but always because they weren't working. Most bipolar drugs didn't work. Bipolar disorder is very difficult to treat because how do you simultaneously treat mania with a depressant and depression with a stimulant? Lithium is a stabilizer that kept my highs from getting too high and my lows from getting too low. Lithium was the only medication that worked for me but I knew I could accomplish the same thing without it and its diarrhea and possible long-term kidney damage. I felt that for the most part I'd been dealing pretty well with my BD for the past few years so I was ready to go drug-free.

The most important thing in being medication-free is to always be aware of where you are. When I'm starting to feel depressed, I try to get out and hang around with friends. When I'm getting manic, I try to channel my energy into making things with my hands. I'm always aware of when I'm getting manic and when I'm feeling depressed and I ride it out like a storm, knowing that, eventually, it will pass. It always does.

As Frank Sinatra put it, it's an 'over-acute capacity for sadness as well as elation.' It's a flood of emotion that will give you the confidence to pursue any crazy idea that pops into your head at two am. It makes you cry just THINKING about a Subaru commercial. It's a hyperactive empathy that makes you wince with physical pain when you see somebody get injured. It sucks. I cried for days after Sandy Hook.

I just read of a study that claims people who were picky eaters as kids grow up to have mental issues. What they should have said was that some people who are extra-sensitive can't stand the textures and certain tastes of things like mushrooms or clams. I'd spend thirty minutes picking out every little piece of mushroom from my mother's tuna casserole no matter how finely she diced it.

We all appreciate the art, music, literature, and religious and political leadership that people who are known or generally assumed to have been manic depressives have contributed for hundreds of years, but we hear the word bipolar and immediately think of irrational behavior and violence. Winston Churchill and Abraham Lincoln most surely suffered serious bipolar depression but kept a steady hand on the tiller during their country's most perilous times.

If you or someone you know may be bipolar, know that Edgar Allan Poe, Kurt Cobain, Isaac Newton, Mozart, Mahatma Ghandhi, Ernest Hemingway, Tim Burton, Jimi Hendrix, Teddy Roosevelt, Brian Wilson, Jackson Pollack, Ted Turner, Vincent Van Gogh, Robin Williams, Virginia Woolf, Sting, Martin Luther King, Job, Plato, Buzz Aldrin, Napoleon Bonaparte, Jim Carey, Ralph Waldo Emerson, Mark Twain, Britney Spears, Sinatra, Agatha Christy, Florence Nightingale, Tom Waits, Friedrich Nietzsche, Abbie Hoffman, Marilyn Monroe, Amy Winehouse, Ludwig Von Beethoven, Edvard Munch, Lyndon B Johnson and Ozzy Osbourne are, or were thought to be, manic depressives. I looked it up.

And more people die of suicide than by homicide in the United States. I looked that up, too.

How to Make a Blowpipe

Needed-
One A nylon tube @ 9"
One C nylon tube @ 8"
Two B nylon spacers @ 2"
One E PVC pipe @ 3 1/2"
One F hose @ 4"

Put the A and C together, leaving one inch of the A sitting out of one end of the C. Next fix the PVC on the flush end but 1 1/4" up like you did with the bottoms. Add some glue and put the hose on the top.

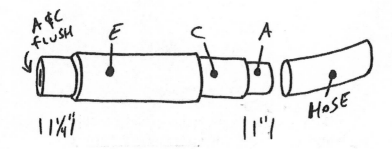

You'll need a flap on the bottom of the blowpipe to keep the air in the bag while you take breaths. You can buy one cheap enough when you get the other bagpipe supplies.

Assemble

Once all of your parts are made, get a large elk skin bag, reeds and a chanter from a bagpipe supply store. A tie-in kit will come with the bag that will show you how to tie the stocks into the bag.

Put a cork in the chanter stock for meditating.

The Long Flight

Kenny and I had just said goodbye to my father and we sat in a bar in Providence's TF Greene airport. A storm was coming in and my Dad dropped us off early so we could catch an earlier flight and make the connection in Newark to get back to Seattle.

I had some mediocre lobster bisque and an over-priced beer. There were about six or eight other people in the bar, among them a cute girl who I would have guessed to be about eighteen, except that she was drinking a beer so she was at least twenty-one. It was a large beer, the same kind I was drinking, so maybe she was twenty-two. Still, she was too young so I tried to avoid eye contact.

They announced something about my flight being cancelled and said everybody had to get up to the counter and get rescheduled. I stood in line and the cute girl queued up behind me.

"Do you think we'll make the 5:30?", she asked me. She was asking about the connection in Newark to Seattle. It had to be the Utilikilt that told her I was going to Seattle and not, say, Cleveland or Kansas City.

When you're a guy over forty you automatically suss out younger women as soon as you meet them. If they're cute and within range then of course you make every attempt to get them into bed. But if they're too young, you put them into a different category. You become a Protector against all those other dirtbag predators who are all over the place and want nothing else but to take advantage of all the pretty young things that are out of your league.

We had about twenty minutes in line and then an hour together in the bar before our plane took off. We hit it off immediately and I could easily picture her as a younger friend. Just a cool girl who, no matter how cute, I would never see naked.

We each had a book to read and we talked about our favorite writers. She said she liked to write poetry and I told her I could only write non-fiction. And crockpot recipes.

I mentioned the cookbook I had started writing and how I was hoping to get it properly published. She told me she had a friend who was an editor of some sort so I gave her a copy of the first draft that I had in my backback to give to him. But I told her "It's really more of a guy's book...", hoping she wouldn't bother to open it.

Her seat on the plane to Newark was in the back and I was more in the middle. I did the Sunday crossword puzzle and wondered what was reading. The book she brought or my stories of casual sex and manic depression?

I got off the plane first and waited for her. The storm stayed east of New York and we had almost two hours before our next flight. We found a Mexican restaurant that claimed to have the Best Guacamole in the Entire United States. Imagine our luck Right here in Newark International Airport!

As we talked and ate and drank, I started to see her a little differently. Turns out she was actually thirty-two and an engineer at Boeing. We talked about religion, relationships, and the hypocrisy of most of the people who go to Burning Man. She had a smile and a laugh that somehow felt very familiar to me. We talked like we'd known each other for years.

And then she asked me if I had really been married for ten years and if I was still friends with Sean. So she HAD pulled out my manuscript and read at least the first two stories. If she stopped there, I felt I might still have a chance with her. You know, I thought of saying, I don't think I want it to be edited after all. And it's really not ready to be read by anybody... But then I figured, fuck it. Either she accepts me or not. No point in postponing the inevitable, if that's what it was.

When it was time to board for home, we walked over to our gate. We passed an international flight that made a last call for Charles D'Gaulle and she asked, "Whaddaya say? Wanna switch flights?"

I seriously thought about it for a second and realized that if it weren't for all the practical reasons like money and the fact that I had a dog that might have to be quarantined or something, I would have gone. And I felt like, had she been serious, we would have had a great time in Paris and something to tell our grandkids.

Just as we got to gate C-25 she said, "Hey! That's you. They just paged you."

I didn't hear it and I wondered how she knew my last name. And then I remembered the manuscript, which had it right on the front cover. The future book, which might possibly guarantee I will never get laid by any English-speaking woman again. Ironic to the extreme, since one of the reasons I wanted to write in the first place was 'cause I thought chicks dig writers. And because if you're a writer it's almost expected that you're a drunk and it's kind of endearing when you make an ass of yourself and have to be wheeled back to your boat in a dock cart. If you've never been published and you act like that, you're just a drunk.

The woman at the gate said that since I was travelling with a pet I shouldn't be sitting by the emergency door over the wing. Normally I would have insisted that Kenny and I were more than ready to help evacuate the plane if we had to make a water-landing in South Dakota, but since I was travelling with my new girlfriend, I just asked if we could sit together.

We had a row of three seats to ourselves, with Kenny in the middle. We both passed on the headphones, preferring to talk rather than watch the movies. It was nice. For a while, anyway.

And then she started asking me questions about the book and I confessed that I wished I hadn't given it to her. She looked surprised and asked me why. I told her I was embarrassed about it and I'd kind of like it if she'd give it back to me. Maybe after we got to know each other better she could read it. Meaning, but not saying, that she could have it back after we've slept together. It's much easier to be open and honest with somebody once you've exchanged bodily fluids with them.

She dismissed that immediately. "I can take it," she said, almost a little defensively. We were both quiet for a little while and then she looked at me as if she was going to say something, and pulled my book out of her bag.

She opened it to where she must have left off and started reading the next story, about the time I fucked a nineteen year old in a hot tub after her uncle had expressly forbidden me not to. It made me very uncomfortable, but all I could do was read along with her and hope it wasn't as bad as I thought it was. When she was done with the story, she put the manuscript on her lap and stared at the cover for a few minutes. I almost told her I was going to leave that story out of the book, but realized it would be best if I just kept my goddamn mouth shut from now on.

She picked up the manuscript again and read and read and read. Some more crockpot recipes, and the 12 Step Program for Christians. I felt like telling her the 12

Step Program wasn't even my idea. It came from Thom, who I worked with briefly at Utilikilts who suggested I do a 12 Step Program and make the last step 'Go Get Drunk'. And as far as the girl in the hot tub goes, well, you know, she had her frigging hand on my pecker the whole time her uncle was in the tub and it was out of respect for him that we waited until everybody else left and what was I supposed to do anyway? NOT fuck her?!?! Be reasonable for Christ's sake!

You know, I almost said, it's pretty easy to judge people by reading their book. Why don't YOU write a goddamn book and let ME read it?

Instead, I said nothing and pretended to read a book. Next was a story called 'Look Alive, Leonard'. All of the stuff in that story are the kinds of things that one would probably not reveal to a potential partner in the first few weeks, or months even, of a new relationship. And of all the stories in the cookbook, this was the one I most wanted back.

I put my book away and pretended to take a nap. I positioned my head in a way that allowed my protruding Cro-Magnon brow to obscure the direction of my left eye. Me sleep now. Me no care what you read.

But really I was reading along with her about my almost identical cousin who killed himself, the deep depression after my buddy Dave died and the full manic pendulum swing that made my wife leave me. Bar fights, more drunken sex, and the general instability that would send any sane woman walking quickly and quietly in the other direction.

She finished the story and put the manuscript back in her bag. And before I could think of a proper thing to say, she turned and raised the visor to look out the window.

I was getting the silent treatment! Sweet, our first fight! I couldn't wait to tell the kids.

When we landed I told her my friend Valerie was waiting for me and that I absolutely insisted that we give her a ride home, even though she said she should take a taxi.

Nonsense! You will come with me and meet the female friend who would do an airport run for me at midnight on a Monday, thereby proving that I must be a good guy.

On the drive from SeaTac to Capital Hill, where she lived, we all made small talk. After we dropped her off, Valerie grilled me about every detail, but I wasn't sure what had just happened. Either I 'met cute' my second wife or learned a valuable lesson about discretion. I had no way of knowing and wouldn't likely know for at least a couple days.

I gave her my business card, which was for custom-made bagpipes that said 'Putting the FUN Back in Funeral' on the back and told her that "This was nice", in the offhanded way that implies, 'Well, I guess I'll talk to you tomorrow.'

She never did call me. We exchanged a couple of emails and she even sent me a book called *Cowboys Are My Weakness* with an inscription that said, 'Maybe this will help you understand women a little better'.

Sure enough, it didn't.

CPSIA information can be obtained
at www.ICGtesting.com
Printed in the USA
FSOW01n1321220717
36403FS